Natural Law, The Zero Point Field,
and the Spirit that is Holy

Natural Law, The Zero Point Field, and the Spirit that is Holy

Dr. H. Lawrence Zillmer

Library of Congress Control Number:		2014916192
ISBN:	Hardcover	978-1-4990-7071-2
	Softcover	978-1-4990-7072-9
	eBook	978-1-4990-7073-6

This book was printed in the United States of America.

NKJV—New King James Version
Scripture taken from the New King James Version. Copyright 1979, 1980, 1982 by Thomas Nelson, inc. Used by permission. All rights reserved.

Rev. date: 10/07/2014

To order additional copies of this book, contact:
Xlibris LLC
1-888-795-4274
www.Xlibris.com
Orders@Xlibris.com
671660

CONTENTS

*"In the beginning God created the heavens and the earth.
And the earth was formless and void, and darkness was
upon the face of the deep; and the Spirit of God moved
over the waters. The God said, "Let there be light, and
there was light." (Genesis 1:1-3)*

*"In the beginning was the Word (the Message from God
via the Messenger from God, Jesus), "and the Word was with
God and the Word was God. This One was in the beginning
with God. All things came into being through Him, and apart
from Him nothing came into being that has come into being.
In Him was life; and the life was the light of mankind. And
the light shines in the darkness; and the darkness could not
overpower it." John 1:1-5*

CHAPTER ONE

The Major Premise:
We are so much more than atoms and molecules

Think of this as a sharing from a bearded veteran of the faith to his fellow sisters and brothers in our mutual exoduses from our Egypts and our Babylons to the Promised Land. We need the truth and empowerment of the Holy Spirit, those pillars of cloud by day and of fire by night for our daily living. Yahweh Jireh, our God Who Provides, has provided the guidance and given us some special insights into the marvelous beauty of His sustaining power and love which we need for today's living. Let us praise our Heavenly Father for His gifts of love and open our hearts of faith for the Bread of Life He provides. Blessed indeed are those whose strength is in the Lord. In whose heart are the highways to Zion. Passing through valleys of sorrow, they make it a place of rejoicing. They grow from strength to strength. All such appear before God in Zion. (Psalm 84:5,6)

We know the problems of today. More Christians have been martyred in the last century than in all previous centuries. We have a government which is trying to take the mention of our Savior Jesus out of the schools and all public meetings. We live among people with a religion which teaches that if anyone kills us they are guaranteed entrance into paradise. Academicians and men of science, out of touch with nature and Natural Law, openly ridicule our saving faith. I could go on and on but that would only give our evil adversary means for boasting.

If that is all there is to life and living I would not be writing this, but there is so much of the love and beauty and truth of our Lord, which responsible research has revealed, that I wish to share some of it. I have been blessed with the best of an education—a PhD from a leading research university, a degree from a responsible Bible college, a lifetime given to study, and a life-long commitment to my Lord. I am neither an alarmist nor one who thinks that positive thinking alone will solve our problems. But because of His love for us, the Spirit of Truth from the One, our Heavenly Father, has provided something special of the "daily bread" for which we pray in our Lord's Prayer. Let us join together and feast upon it "in the presence of those who trouble us." (Psalm 23:5)

Three streams, one river!

This "feasting," which I wish to discuss, is a unique combination of three avenues of truth into one stream never available before in such a manner. From four centuries of scientific investigation we know more about Natural Law and how it impinges upon our daily living than ever before. From Quantum Mechanics, especially the field of Biophysics, we have learned something about the energy fields and how they operate in life giving light energy in our portion of the Zero Point Field. Due to research and some rethinking we now know what the Message of Jesus was as it was released as The Way in that first century of our time before it got clouded in the activities of the Reformation and the years of action and reaction since. We are now able to put these three avenues of reality into a single stream. Let those closing verses of the book of Revelation be the invitation: "The Spirit and the Bride say, 'Come.' They who hear let them say, 'Come.' Let the one who is thirsty come; let the one who wishes take of the waters of life without cost." (Revelation 22:17)

King of kings and Lord of lords

Key to it all, key to our faith, is to recognize the fact that through it all, Jesus Christ is still King of kings and Lord of lords. Too often we want a king, like the king that first Palm Sunday crowd wanted, and when they realized Jesus was not going to be that kind of king, Judas betrayed Him, Peter denied Him and the crowd crucified Him. Yet He is a king, a king of truth and righteousness, as He told Pilate. (John 18;36, 37)

Jesus does rule this troubled world. How? With the rod of iron: What we sow we shall reap. If we sow in the flesh, we shall of the flesh reap corruption; if we sow in the Spirit we shall of the Spirit reap eternal life. Every human is either on the Narrow Way of Life or the Broad Highway of nothingness and lies which leads to death. We are either journeying by faith out of the slavery of our Egypts and the worldliness of our Babylons, or we remain in the processes and procedures of those who will not attempt the spiritual journey of life. Given the condition of our world at this moment, the Broad Highway is heavily populated! Why?

A world of atoms and molecules

We discovered the world is made up of atoms and molecules. We discovered the Periodic Table of chemistry. We learned about the laws of astronomy! We discovered economic laws, something of the world of psychology and how to treat diseases and cure medical problems. And we were foolish enough to think that such knowledge was all that mattered! It all began over four centuries ago.

In the Seventeenth Century Rene Descartes and too many of the scientists who followed him, conceived the idea that humans existed through their mental processes, "I think, therefore I am." He had a vision that this world was one vast machine which could be understood through the laws of chemistry, physics and the other sciences. If we know how the machine works, then, through education, we can fix any problem! Add to that Darwin's survival of the fittest and we have a recipe for our current disaster.

Attitudes of materialism, reductionism and random selection

Attitudes of materialism, reductionism and random selection helped set up the world conditions in which we now live. Let me explain!

Those who focus on <u>materialism</u> perceive no need for any spiritual considerations as being necessary for living well. If we have sufficient food, shelter and clothing and a little, or much, pleasure, what further need do we have? The Jesus statement that man does not live by bread alone but by the words that proceed from the Heavenly Father (Matthew 4:4) is completely discounted.

If the world is conceived as being only a material machine, then it can be <u>reduced</u> to its parts, examined, and those parts, when reassembled correctly, make for a smooth running machine! According to the reductionists, any part of this world can be studied by understanding how it is made. To fix anything, take it apart, find what's wrong and reassemble it correctly! To study medicine, study a cadaver, learn its parts and one is ready to doctor living ill people!

But living beings are more than the sum of their parts. Holistic medicine tries to include the spiritual, the more-than-physical, in treating ill people since they believe that life is more than an assemblage of its parts. A dead robin is no longer a living robin although all the physical parts remain in the body! The aura of life has departed.

But how did this physical assemblage happen? Those who believe that plants and animals evolved through <u>random selection</u> believe that new beings happen by accident and survival of the fittest. In the course of generations, from time to time a superior being comes into existence. The new being becomes dominant through being better suited to survive than the original. Given time, these people believe, through accident and the survival of the fittest, life evolved from an amoeba to human kind.

In the reality of life, a horse mated to a donkey produces a new species, a mule, but it is infertile. Such facts are simply ignored. We observe that animals and plants which deviate from the parental norm are usually ostracized and die.

Materialism, reductionism and random selection, though contrary to simple reality, when empowered by the idea of survival of the fittest, have become the foundation of current understandings of who and what we humans are. Who needs a Creator when we know how everything happened and we are convinced we know that which works best for the survival of the species? We can figure it out, work out the details and fix any problems, thus allowing the best adjusted to dominate the upward climb from the one celled amoeba! Simple, neat, but not only a lie but the reason for the amoral chaos that seems to run the ways and means of too many humans today! Who needs the spiritual to cloud up what we believe to be modern progressive reality? If we can just find life on another planet that would prove our theory of random selection!

Quantum Mechanics

But our Creator and Redeemer is not finished with the human race. As we get to know more about this world into which we were born, new truths add to new understandings so that what was once a matter of spiritual faith lived and taught by spiritual people, is now a matter of beautiful reality.

The pioneers of Quantum Mechanics, in the arena of biophysics, have explored what has been termed the Zero Point Field, that field of energy which encompasses and expedites life on earth, particularly among and within humans. It is the avenue by which our Creator and Sustainer brings all that we know into order and harmony. That which was and is a matter of faith, and a faith too often very poorly explained by churchmen, is now an open door to experience the depths and riches of this Creation in which we live.

The invitation

I invite the reader and those who wish to "behold the beauty of the Lord and meditate in His temple" (Psalm 27:4), to journey with me into a new set of horizons which our Good Shepherd desires to lead us—the green pastures and the still waters of life which are life indeed.

Let us join together with our forebearers of the faith, Abraham and Sarah, and walk the covenant God gave them: If they would leave their country and their kindred and their father's house (their comfort zone) and would go to a land God would show them (when they arrived!), He would bless them and they would be a blessing. (Genesis 12:1f)

We have developed the tools of logic and scientific analysis suitable for this venture. We have the invitation of Jesus, "When the Holy Spirit comes He will lead you into all truth and bring to your remembrance all that I have spoken to you." (John 14:26) Indeed, our Creator has given us a developed frontal lobe of our brain for just such a function, why not use it?

It is best to read this presentation in sequence for it has a line of argument which begins with our recognition of who and what we humans are and how we can live well during our brief sojourn upon this earth. It will end with new horizons of beautiful realistic potentials that actually work. Let's take our common sense with us, look objectively at our life and living, and enjoy the journey begun so long ago with Abraham and Sarah. We will be part of the multitudes who have followed this attitude of adventure into the richness of this creation; journeying out of the slavery of our Egypts and the worldliness of our Babylons as our forefathers of the faith did so long ago. We are never alone in this journey of life unless we choose to be. We have our Good Shepherd to lead us, our indwelling Holy Spirit to guide and empower us and the ministering angels to assist us. Our Father provides for us. New horizons of our Creator's goodness, love and truth await us.

The reality of Natural Law

We need to begin with the reality of Natural Law, the laws which govern and give meaning to the daily experiences in which we live. When we weren't able to "get" the meaning of this creation, God gave us the Ten Commandments, which are but ten simple statements explaining the moral dimension of Natural Law. We will explore this in depth in the next chapter.

We will find in our interactions with natural life, out in the fields and woods of living plants and animals, fish and birds, models for human living. Those laws are best experienced where least touched by humans. It is our fear of nature, our ignorance of its laws and purposes, which have contributed so much to the current mess we are in. Let us return to our natural foundations and look at life about us, simply and persistently.

The problem of language

But as we revisit nature let us remember a human phenomenon— we view it all through the language with which we think and with which we communicate. To that extent, thinking, which is based upon language, does construct a system of virtual reality of what we think actually exists! But what happens to those virtual realities when our mind returns with our body to the elements? We are so much more than a machine guided by materialism, reductionism and random selection. What about our spiritual essence, our soul?

The key to understanding and living well is the recognition of the spiritual dimension of our life. It is our spiritual essence, that which has been called our soul, which will journey into the Spiritual World. If we reduce ourselves into a thinking mechanism, then we have left out that which makes us uniquely human, what is the actual me. If we are only a machine, death is an absolute finality; it is the end!

To help us deal with this special human essence, which the Bible describes as the breath of God, our Creator provided the Holy Spirit of Truth, which dwells within the unconscious of every human. It exists to guide and empower us for better living. This will be the focus of Chapter Four.

Spiritual reality

Here is where we part with so many—we accept this spiritual reality, this spiritual dimension of our lives, whereas so many don't. We who have sought out and committed ourselves to this truth know its reality. We experience it daily, even hourly. It is the way of love and beauty and the truth for living well. Those who will not accept this spiritual dimension in their lives will never know its reality. With absolute conviction, they will deny that which doesn't, for them exist, and it truly doesn't, for them! The language with which they think simply doesn't include this phenomenon!

The major premise

This is then the major premise: We are so much more than a mind and a machine-like body. Responsible modern research has opened new doors of understanding as to how this Creation works, together with a new awareness of the Intelligence that made and sustains it all. Jesus did say that He was the Bread of Life that they who come to Him would never hunger, that they who believed in Him would never thirst. (John 6:35) Let's do some feasting!

Do not worry if these ideas are Methodist, Lutheran, Roman Catholic or Orthodox. Due to modern research we know what the ancient church taught before the modern denominations began to form in the 16th Century. The theology of this study is based upon the church teachings in the beginning of the church's existence. A good introduction is Justo Gonzales' book "Christian Thought Revisited."

The one eternal truth

The truth we seek is the ever present, unchanging, eternal truth from the One. We can look at human history and objectively examine the contributions and fallacies of mankind down through the centuries. We can objectively look at what has worked and what has not worked. We can recognize how materialism, reductionism and random selection have contributed to the mess in which we find ourselves. Survival of the fittest usually means that those who will use brute force and cunning manipulations believe they will end up the winners. The Samsons and the Jezebels lose on the long run! Such "achievers" do not leave behind workable solutions to the truth of life!

It is time to listen to what has worked every time it is tried—the voice of the Holy Spirit, the life and teachings of Jesus and the witness of the Natural World, the work of the Holy Trinity. It is time to tune into the Spiritual World and pay attention to what it says. Amazingly enough most people choose to go their own way rather than what has worked every time anyone has committed to it. Human will! I will do it my own way! The forbidden fruit will make me as wise as God. (Eve) You aren't the king I wanted! (Judas) And so it goes. But it need not!

We are to be the "called out ones." Unless we make a deliberate and continual choice, we will slide on through life, never allowing the spiritual dimension of our existence, which alone will journey into the spiritual world when our bodies return to the dust, to develop. We are either journeying on the spiritual Way of Life as lived and taught by Jesus or we are not!

Religion and science

We have perhaps come to a time when the best of science and the best of spiritual thinking can be joined into a unity reflecting the Source, the Unity and the Intelligence of the One, in whose creation we find ourselves. For too long we have been in one of two camps, either in the camp called "science" or the camp called "religion." We have been refighting the ancient antagonism between what is perceived as one set of understandings of our world and what is believed to be an opposite concept of how-it-is.

When the sound and the fury have mitigated a little we remember that there is only one earth and one set of rules, although there are many human perspectives on those rules and their meaning. We are one human race, one flock in one pasture, although we may wish it were not so at times!

In our walk with Jesus we have come to savor the spiritual dynamic of the faith walk based upon love. We have experienced in bits and pieces the potential of the Message Jesus brought from Heaven to Earth. We have tasted the appetizers, we are being led into a banquet as were our forebearers of the faith, Abraham and Sarah.

Our human spiritual journey

The human spiritual inquiry goes back far beyond any and all holy books. To engage in the search for spiritual reality is to be human. What is the purpose of our existence? Science presumes and we have long recognized that a singular system of reality exists— Natural Law. To know it and live by its parameters is to live well in this environment in which we find ourselves. There is Truth, a uniting and singular truth transcending all human ideas of what is considered truth. It exists whether we personally believe it or not, whether we accept it or not! It is Natural Law. We know instinctively that to recognize this Law and practice it is to live well. It is part of the goodness of our human ability to learn, to analyze, to awaken to larger realities.

Let us begin all our searches for truth with this reality—the laws exist. If we would live well we must live by those rules. Here science has served us well. We have volumes of technical books on every subject from Astronomy to Zoology!

But more than that, we have our indwelling Holy Spirit, given to us to guide us into all truth and empower us for living in harmony with that truth. We have the potential of allowing the glorious truths of the One, the Intelligence, the Loving Fellow Traveler into our troubled and messed up lives. The answers are here. We who are on this pilgrimage have tasted the appetizers of love and beauty and harmony and peace. We have been given a new lease on possibilities for living. The old order has spent itself. A new world beckons.

It is an inadequate knowledge and the unwillingness to accept that which builds the harmonies of this creation of law and order into a splendid unity which has caused so many of our problems. For too long we have allowed the city dwellers, the laboratory technicians and the entrenched academicians, even atheists, define light and life and love. It is time to take a loving look at the plants, the herbs, the fish and the birds and the animals—it is time to take a new look at ourselves. It is time to truly perceive ourselves in the wider vistas of our Good shepherd. There is so much more. There is always so much more!

Our journey is more than a faith journey, although faith in the worth of the journey is essential for it to be of real worth to any individual. This journey is of experiences, of encounters, of mysteries and beauty for those who will simply live out their day by day experiences in the larger light of the forests, fields, lakes and mountains about us as we are sustained by the loving Will of love from our Creator and the One who wishes to be our Friend and Shepherd. Let us further examine this foundation.

A Meditation

Dear Lord, Creator and the Intelligence
    By which all that is has come into being
What wonders you have placed about and within me!
Forgive me for the too many times I have viewed the mechanism
    And not seeing the larger reality

That my understanding of a portion of life
       Was assumed to be all there is
Lord, I am hungry for the Bread of sustaining truth
       By Your grace I have found the life You offer in Jesus
       I rejoice in my citizenship in the spiritual World
       I have feasted so often on Your manna of truth
         Contained in Your blessed revelations
Given to me by Jesus, Your messenger from Heaven
       Through the Holy Spirit of truth
Thank You, blessed Father
       For the grace and strength to leave the slavery of my Egypts
         To reject the worldliness of my Babylons
           To be a called out one
       Forgive the attitudes and darkness remaining within me
         I pray for the discernment and the commitment
           To lay them aside
       To replace them with attitudes and acts of goodness
       To walk with You in the Spirit and in Truth
         Into new vistas of Your beauty
I can lay the lesser behind me
       And by Your grace
         I can turn new pages of my life's living
       And experience something of
         Those new and blessed vistas
       Your Will has placed before and within me
         For every moment of my daily living
Lead me humbly and gently into the realities of Natural Law
       May those precepts be a light unto my feet
         And a lamp unto my path
This moment of my living
       And for all eternity.

CHAPTER TWO

The Foundation For Living Well—Natural Law

The great gift of science to our understanding of this world in which we find ourselves is the discovery of the principles and order of Natural Law, the rules and the order upon which our world operates and the intellectual discipline necessary to discover and record those facts. The rules are all about us but too often we are so removed from the natural world that they are taken for granted, seem incomprehensible, even dangerous to us. It was not always so.

Our prehistoric ancestors learned the rules early in life. They either learned them and followed them or they did not survive! What will we do, what have we done, with the information we now have? Will we survive? Have we so surfeited ourselves in human virtual understandings that we can no longer perceive the reality of Natural Law? If we will not yield our human biases to reality there is little possibility for us to find the truth of our environment, which we need for living well.

Beginning with Descartes

So far Descartes was right; this world is somewhat like a machine in its vast connections and interconnections. But there is more to it than that—there is the world of Quantum Mechanics and what has been termed the Zero Point Field, which will be the focus of Chapter Three. There are the spiritual realities which govern and sustain everything as discussed above.

Much of Natural Law is visible to our human senses in the natural world about us; enough so that if we really saw it we would have all the information we need for living well. Primitive man knew there was much more to life and living than what they could see with the physical eye; that dealing well with the unseen was essential to living well in what is seen. Would that modern man had so much sense!

We, in our laboratory knowledge of our physical world, have lost this perspective of our dependency upon the spiritual to live well in the physical. Rather, too many have rejected it as primitive, unnecessary for modern technological living. This current view of how-it-is has allowed us to create this mess we live in today. We should have discovered that our simple paradigm of this world is unrealistic, there has to be more. We need a better understanding. And that better understanding is beckoning us today. It all begins with a larger view of Natural Law.

Natural Law, a larger view

Natural Law is simply the order of the behavior patterns of all that exists. All matter in this world operates under laws of order which produce the harmony that unites the systems into one cohesive unit—our Creator's Will.

We have learned through disciplined scientific studies in Quantum Mechanics that we humans can influence matter at a distance through our will. I will delve into this more thoroughly in the next chapter. Sufficient to say that if human wills can influence matter, certainly the divine omnipotent, omnipresent and omniscient Will can do so!

Only one system

There is but one such unity existing everywhere and in all time. Every human exists within the confines of Natural Law, is bound by it and must live in harmony with it if they would live at all, even though they may never have heard of it!

This has nothing to do with human laws, or worse, many times nothing to do with what we think are those laws! No congress enacted them. No dictator invented them. They were in operation long before humans arrived on the scene and will be here after the last human disappears. We have discovered that within parameters we can use them for our various purposes. But in order to live well in this environment we need to realize that Natural Law exists, controls us, is part of every moment of our living and we flaunt it to our disaster.

But we must not stop where the ancient Stoic masters stopped— that nature is all there is, that it is the laws of nature which are the ultimate power. Just as the Stoic philosophers were reacting to the practices of religious leaders geared to their own profit, so we too are sometimes repelled by what passes as religious leadership. Those who should be leading us into the adventure of Abraham and Sarah, the leaving of our fixed human ideas of how it is into the vistas of reality the Holy Spirit has for each of us, are, by their simple and stubborn reliance on fixed traditional language structures are too often actually blocking and hindering this spiritual adventure.

Natural Law and Human belief systems

We have lived in human groupings so long that we have come to believe that whatever our nation, our city, our family, ourselves and especially our religious leaders believe, is the way it is. We have the current messes within our selves and our societies, and the too often the silence or rantings from the pulpits, to demonstrate the folly of such simple assumptions. If we want to learn how to live via the laws under which we live, spend some time in the wilderness! Jesus did! Moses did! Paul did! Francis of Assisi did!

Nowhere is the distance between Natural Law and current religious beliefs better illustrated than in the controversy over homosexuality. There is no need for the Bible or any other religious book to warn of its fallacy—it is contrary to Natural Law. If homosexuality was practiced by everyone, the human race would disappear in one generation! Homosexual unions deprive the partners of the simple fact that the anima and the animus, the female and the maleness of humanity, are designed to interact and build both partners into a unity impossible in homosexual unions where neither the uniqueness of each sex is understood nor the potential for wholeness possible.

Whatever linguistic arguments are proposed, and human imaginations are capable of amazing constructs, Natural Law is the way it is. Let's accept this and live by it. Above all, let's hear it stated simply and lovingly from the pulpits! Everyone has their major temptations, some this and some that, but let's recognize any behavior contrary to the Will of the Intelligence who made this Creation and then, through the grace, strength and wisdom of the Holy Spirit, build our lives in accordance with that Will.

Cycles of existence

Every living entity, even non-living entities, have a cycle of existence. We live in daily, weekly, monthly, seasonally, yearly, etc. cycles. All cycles have a beginning, a growing, and aging and an ending so a new cycle can begin. Human time lines, calendars, are human concoctions, they do not exist in real time. Calendar reality is based on a human arrangement, it is a virtual reality. Therefore, whatever reality we give it in no way influences or controls Natural Law! We have a system based upon the supposed birth of Jesus. Other cultures have other calendars, all based, of necessity, upon some beginning. Rome's was based upon the supposed founding of Rome.

Ancient calendars based upon cycles of living were cumbersome and confusing. Any one cycle overlaps other cycles. A unified calendar is needed for simplification. Such a calendar is useful as long as we don't think of it as based upon Natural Law.

Each of us has been on this island home for so many trips about the sun, so many turns upon the earth's axis. That it has names given it by the Mayan, the Christian or the Chinese calendars is relevant only to the given cultures. How we measure the entropy, the declining energy of our life cycle, is a matter of human relevance—whatever system of measurement used in no way interferes or changes the trips around the sun or the turnings upon the earth's axis. This reality is key to understanding our situation in this world in which we find ourselves.

We have thought of ourselves as onlookers, evaluators and judges, an unnecessary adjunct in the vast flow of existence. As we shall see, that is not a true picture. But in order to put our existence in its proper place, we must recognize that Natural Law, including the discoveries of Quantum Mechanics, exists, runs this world and all that is in it, including each of us. To live well is to live in harmony with those laws.

Our personal mind set

Each of us is a finite being set without our choices in the cycles of existence about and within us. We didn't invent those cycles. We didn't choose our parents, our genetic code, our physical characteristics or our economic status. We arrived on the scenario of life with them! We are simply part of them whether we choose to be or not, unless we opt out by suicide—always a possibility, whether actively or passively!

To live is to be part of the life of this existence. To live well is to live in harmony with the rest of this existence. To know what that is, we need to be a humble listener, a learner, an adventurer. There is so much that we do not know, so much we cannot know unless we have an open attitude, unless we are teachable. Our attitudes are key to it all. It is the first of the "Blessed attitudes," the Beatitudes, listed by Jesus. "Blessed are the humble, the teachable, for theirs is the Kingdom of Heaven." (Matthew 5:3)

We have the ability to learn. We can learn how to discipline that learning so that what we learn may come close to reality, for it is only the tenets of reality that can form a worthwhile foundation for the choices we must make in our daily living. This avenue is closed to too many people when they attempt to understand the unknown. The great enemy to understanding truth is bias. There is that maxim:

information stimuli in, processed through residual garbage, and you have garbage out!

Our personal attitudes

Since it is ourselves who are the seekers; our attitudes, our limitations of learning, our ability to be open minded, along with the attitude of being a true seeker, will determine what we perceive to be reality. Every incoming stimuli is screened and selections made by us as to what will be perceived and added into our cognitive realities and what will be sloughed off as irrelevant—what will be part of the language of our thinking and what won't be. However essential some information may be for our well being, if it is not deemed important, it is simply ignored! No human is impervious to this coloration of their thinking processes. It is impossible to process all the stimuli coming into ourselves from our physical senses. We can and do select whatever we think is relevant to our needs. What we select becomes our version of reality.

It is obvious that those with the language skills, the humility and the attitudes of exploration are the ones who will journey furthest in this inquiry so essential to human well being—the daily journey with the Holy Spirit and the Spiritual World. Blessed indeed are the humble and the teachable by the Spirit that is Holy, for they have a chance to perceive and learn reality!

Humility! We must avoid the pitfalls of solipsism! That is, believing something to be true because we believe it is!

Our history

A good antidote is history. We humans have been here for many millenniums. The human race has experienced so much, if we will but learn from it. That is why we expect our children to study history.

Each of us has a personal history. A giant step forward in our knowledge of Natural Law occurred when ten key issues, ten commandments, were codified. As given to us via Moses, they are ten simple statements of principles, commandments given to us by our Creator, so that we might be better able to live within Natural Law—five relating to the larger spiritual world and five therefore principles derived from those preceding five. The reality of these Ten Commandments is all about us in Natural Law. Let us look at those principles.

The Ten Commandments

Originally most were stated in the negative—as thou shalt nots! Primitive people, like children, pay more attention to emphatic negatives! But in order to understand what we are to do after we have avoided the negatives, we need some positive directions as well! They are brief, terse statements since they were chiseled on two tablets of stone which Moses was capable of carrying! They are recorded in Exodus 20:1-17 and Deuteronomy 5:6-21.

Principle One. "You shall have no other Gods before Me." You shall not have any other God but the One who actually made this creation! There is only one set of rules by which this world operates. Wherever one goes, in whatever time period, the rules are the same. It is the basis of all science. Learn the set of rules by which chemistry, astronomy, physics, biology and psychology operate and then live in harmony with them. Why? So we can live well, a basic principle which is explored in the next chapter on the Zero Point Field.

Principle Two. "You shall not make for yourselves an idol." Do not make any human substitutes for those laws. Any substitution is but replacing reality with a nothingness. This is an important premise of all real scientific inquiry. No bias! Only the reality of what is! That is the name by which the Deity identified Himself Moses—I Am— that which is! What else could make more sense or better define the

Intelligence which made and sustains this order in which we live? It is, all else is derivative.

Principle Three. "Do not take the name of the Lord in vain!" The name given the Lord in the Bible, stated in Hebrew, is Yahveh Jireh, the Deity Who Provides. (Genesis 22:14) God has provided the truth we need for living well. What God has provided—don't count as nothing! We have the truth in the Natural Law basis of our environment, in the life and teachings of Jesus, which are totally based upon Natural Law, and in the interior voice of conscience, the Holy Spirit, which speaks reality. What that member of the Holy Trinity always speaks is in harmony with Natural Law and the Jesus development of those laws. We will focus on this in Chapter Four.

Principle Four. "Remember the Sabbath Day and keep it holy!" We must take time out from the stress, the cacophony and our daily tides of living in order to understand the spiritual dimensions of our living if we are ever to make more sense out of this life than a chimpanzee or a robin. We have been given a highly developed frontal lobe in our brain. Let us use this gift to understand what we need to know and to understand if we are to live in harmony with this creation, so that our spiritual essence may develop, so that we might become a spiritual entity capable of living in the Spiritual world.

Principle Five. "Honor your father and mother that you may live long in the land which the Lord your God has given you." That is, respect and honor our parentage. We have a history in the lives and learning of our forebearers all the way back to Adam and Eve—let us honor and learn from what worked for them. We don't need to reinvent the wheel! We are special, unique, one of a kind in our Creator's eyes. We have our Heavenly Father, our Lord Jesus, the Holy Spirit and the ministering Angels to help us find the special truth as to how we are uniquely designed to fit into the celestial chorus.

Principle Six. "You shall do no murder!" This is the first of the five spiritual principles which relate to human living. It begins, as it must, with life itself. Life is a gift set in the midst of life all about us from the ocean depths to beyond the mountain peaks, from our developmental past to our present existence. Life is part of the various energy fields all about and within us. Every human is an integral part of the larger whole. We have learned that ninety per cent of our DNA comes from the "lower" animals. Our need is to honor, care for and allow love relationships to develop. Our loving care allows us to maintain the laws and equilibrium within our environmental world and ourselves.

Every life is a potential for magnificence. Each living entity exists in its own special way. To abort life is to make that journey impossible—which cuts to the very reason for human existence. It is the plan of our Creator that each of us is designed to grow into something unique and special. Killing that life is to destroy the possibility of that potential. Is there a greater crime against the loving energy flow from the Sustainer of our life?

Principle Seven. "You shall not commit adultery!" In order for the human species to develop well it needs to nurture succeeding generations—it needs strong families based upon love. Adultery destroys the family core—the special male and female bonding.

As indicated above, every human male and female, the animus and the anima, has half of the story of life. A strong mutual love bond facilitates personal development if it gives of itself for the spiritual welfare of another. Fornication, using sex as the bonding element between the animus and the anima before the marriage commitment, short circuits real development, real understandings of the other. Human love bondings are so much more than sex! Homosexuality places the potential development of the anima and the animus beyond possibility—the component parts of such unions will never understand either themselves or the wholeness possible in hetero-sexual bondings. Families based upon the true love foundation are essential for the continuation and development of human society generation after generation.

Principle Eight. "You shall not steal!" All humans have a greater or lesser amount of time, energy and possessions. To take what belongs to another, whether a baby or a millionaire, the self-worth of a young man or woman or the material possessions of anyone, is to abuse one's personal stewardship. Stealing, if universally allowed, would make stewardship responsibility impossible. We can exist well only when our stewardship responsibilities are respected and used to their fullest.

Principle Nine. "You shall not bear false witness." You shall not lie! Either a situation, a verbal statement, an affirmation or any verbal construct conforms to reality or it doesn't. If it conforms, then it is useful for building relationships and stewardships, if it doesn't, then it contributes to chaos. Order, harmony and truth are essential for living in peace and love. Engaging or utilizing a lie, which is a nothingness, in the place of reality, makes order impossible. All lies always contribute to chaos, the antithesis of the Creator's Will.

Principle Ten. "You shall not covet!" To covet what is another's is to reject whatever unique personal characteristics one possesses in favor of some supposed advantage possessed by another. Everyone is unique, one of a kind. No clones in our Creator's world!

Our uniqueness, our special contribution, if developed, leads to a wholeness within the individual and within the larger social groups about us. To lose that personal contribution is to deplete any wholeness. The "wholeness" is not a reduction but a beautiful consummation, a holiness, only possible when everyone contributes their unique potentials to the larger whole. Whether little or much, each is essential! The unity of diversity! This begins, of necessity, within ourselves but extends, as we shall see, to the outermost limits of the Zero Point Field, to the ultimate connectedness of all.

It is the ultimate goal of the Holy Spirit, our Holy Paraclete, to guide and empower us into the fulfillment of our specialness. Our faith, our love, our joy is our special kind of faith, love and joy, a unity of our uniqueness with the special love-bond of our Heavenly Father. That is why we have a special name! (Revelation 2:17, 3:12)

These principles, simplified into the base ten of our numbering system, five for the digits of each hand, make it easy to remember. But why do we need to be reminded in order to remember? They are all about us in the natural world for any who will take the time to see and observe.

Our need for the Commandments

The idea that if we don't know them we don't need to follow them, or we would not be judged by them, verges on the ridiculous. There are some who think that if they are removed from courtroom walls, from plaques and printings, they don't need to obey them! To once more state the obvious, the Ten Commandments are but simplified expressions of Natural Law. They exist whether we like them or not. They are not an expression of some culture, although the culture that discovered them is to be commended for their perspicuity. They are stated directives derived from Natural Law.

We need to read, see and live them so we can make conscious decisions to live in harmony with the laws upon which this world is based; so we wouldn't, through rebellion or ignorance, contribute to the destructiveness in this world and thereby cause chaos. We need them because of human blindness. We need them in order to recognize the why of the just consequences of our sins!

This is our island home. In a sense we are trapped here. We are not going to travel to some distant planet to populate it after we have ruined this place we call earth! Isn't it the better part of common sense to live in harmony with the rules of this world? Although we didn't invent Natural Law we are certainly subject to it. To mess up our nest makes no sense at all.

Judgmental Consequences

The Orderer, the Law Maker, the Intelligence who made this world and the principles upon which it operates, cannot tolerate lawbreakers. If anyone, spiritual or human, turns a blind eye to law breaking, allowing it to happen, they become part of the lawbreaking, they contribute to the chaos, they sin against the order itself!

But some will say this order evolved out of beneficial, lucky accident! Never in all of our human history has order come out of chaos without the hand of intelligence. Chaos, left to chaos, only devolves into further chaos. But whether one accepts the principle of an Order-maker in order to have order; the principle is everywhere present in this world in which we live—ask any housewife or farmer! It takes expenditure of intelligence and a working hand to maintain order! There is the need for a constant and necessary flow of constructive energy in this world if we are going to maintain order in what is. Either we commit to it or we are part of the problem!

No responsible person would leave stem cell research to develop by lucky accident! It is the principle of order-making necessary for order, which we observe when we understand the laws which are attached to every part of this world in which we find ourselves and attempt to live in harmony with them. But there is an even larger dimension to this order.

As mentioned above, we know that the vast preponderance of the matter that exists in this creation is invisible; maybe as much as eighty per cent or more. This is not just speculation! We know there is something that binds the entities of this cosmos, stars, planets, comets, etc. together that is more than gravity. It is estimated that the mass of this creation could be compressed into something very small. There is that which binds this creation into a unity that we experience every day and it is more than mechanical gravity. The attraction of the sun's mass is inadequate to keep ex-planet Pluto in place or the return of comets from the distant Kuiper Belt.

There are those who say this existence is only a virtual reality existing in human minds. This world existed long before humans arrived and, at the rate we are going, will be around long after the last human will have destroyed him or her self! There is an I Am and we can only live well if we live within the harmonies of what that I Am has given us! Human imaginations can create many language entities which have no reality beyond the cognition of the human creator. There is nothingness (A) and there is the reality of Natural Law (B). A is never B but B can defuse and delete A's existence. However, A can never make B non-existent.

But what holds all this together? What makes it function so well? Scientists have searched for some particle, some physical entity which make the order possible. Nothing! They are looking in the wrong direction! If the reality of the One is not accepted, then the search for ultimate reality is not going to find much! Looking for life in a dead fish is ridiculous!

Human will and the divine Will

We are beginning to realize that human beings can will events in another's mind, recognize mental influences, be aware of places and events which are not immediately visible and influence physical matter. The experience of human wills influencing events and persons separated in space has been amply tested by solid research. A report of much of that research is documented in Lynne McTaggart's book, "The Field."

Since the order of this creation was established by Intelligence, isn't it the Will of that Intelligence which sustains the order? Isn't that simple common sense? If finite human wills can do it, why can't the Infinite? How is that Will exercised? Through the Zero Point Field, which will be discussed in detail in the next chapter.

What is possible between humans through concentration is certainly possible by the Ultimate Will! Research in the arena of human mental processes, of the influence of human will, its potential and its possibilities, is but an introduction to the Will of the Intelligence which made this world in the first place and sustains it at this present moment. We pray that we will choose to be a part of this Will in every moment of our living, our Existential Nows, every time we say the Lord's Prayer. "Your Kingdom come, Your will be done, on earth as it is in Heaven."

God's Will, God's Plan

We have difficulty distinguishing between the Deity's Will and His Plan. It is like the building of a house. The blueprint is the Plan. The Bible lays out this Plan that God has for human salvation. (John 3:3, 5, 6, 16 for instance) But the order of the Plan exists whether we recognize it or not, read about it in the Bible, or not!

The day by day working out of this Plan, in the lives and purposes of people as they relate to themselves and the rest of this creation, is part of God's sustaining Will, part of the all sustaining energy flowage which is directed through the Zero Point Field in accordance with Natural Law. We break our connection with that Will when we disobey the Commandments, the expression of Natural Law. We cannot destroy this Will, it is part of that which is omnipotent, omniscient and omnipresent. We can only block our personal conformity to that Will. Hence we pray the Lord's Prayer often and mean it!

God does not ordain our human response to His Will. We choose and we become what we choose. But, when and if we break that Will, He, of necessity, exacts the consequences through His creation! If He didn't provide consequences for us, He becomes part of the law breakage!

If God willed our choices then He is responsible for the breakage—let Him punish the law breaker, Himself! Preposterous! God has the blueprint, the Plan for the salvation available for those who choose to accept and walk it. God's Will is expressed in the moment by moment expressions of Natural Law and in the situations He places before us for our spiritual growth and development. How we relate to that Will in our moment by moment situations, what we chose to do, how we choose to live, is our responsibility!

Our Existential Now

We exist in a moment by moment now, the Existential Now. There is only this moment for any human in the realities of Natural Law, which includes the Zero Point Field. If we can think of this experience existing at this moment in the virtual reality of human imaginations, why is it so difficult to place this choice factor in the realm of our relationship with the Infinite? But what difference does it make whether this is true?

Everything! What would happen if we humans realized and recognized the sustaining order of the Will of love and goodness? What if we saw ourselves as entities which are part of a universal whole yet especially expressed in our personal uniqueness? We are special, as every entity is special, within a unified and diverse wholeness. What if we truly realized the love-based Unity of Reality which transcends any human construct of how-it-is? What if we recognized our moral necessity of learning how to live in greater harmony with the absolute order in which we find ourselves? What if we realized the role of law breakage in our capacity for both our spiritual and physical development? What if we recognized that the Jesus message of love and truth leading to harmony is the way it is and would then commit ourselves to His Way of Life through love? What if we took time to study and learn the implications of the Zero Point Field, since it is shared by every cell, as a potential for human relationships?

Sin

But too often we don't take the time to consider these possbilities. There is a condition in human living which we call sin. Every human has attitudes, mind-sets, which can lead to acts of rebellion, of willful disobedience, of willful non-compliance. Every human child learns the formula of obedience to the big people and getting the cookies or disobedience and no cookies! The above-mentioned Ten Commandments were given to us so we could recognize our sins— our disobedience to the underlying rules that sustain this creation, and recognizing them, do something about them beginning with our attitudes. We can handle this situation in several ways.

We can say that everyone sins and therefore it doesn't matter. Every disobedience disturbs the personal energy field about and within us. Sin matters; it always matters. It always affects the participant's energy field since sin blocks the incoming Will of the love light energy. Less light and energy is always less light and energy in our personal energy field than what could and should be. There is an inevitable shrinkage of our personal energy field due to attitudes of anger, hatred, lust, and especially lying. There is an expansion of our personal aura when it is fueled by love, joy, peace, etc., the fruit of the work of the Holy Spirit.

False paradigms, virtual realities

We can imagine a different paradigm of how-it-is in our relationship with the One, the absolute Intelligence. Gurus, by the untold hordes, have constructed virtual realities that claim various ways and means of keeping the Intelligence happy. How is it possible that what they propose will actually keep Him or Her happy if it is contrary to what fuels the energy field of light, the universal energy field the Intelligence created and sustains?

Obviously the only way to please the Creator is to live in harmony with that Field of Natural Law. We will be blessed and develop spiritually and physically by allowing the light energy of love to flow from the Sustainer into our being. Either we do it or we don't. To say this or that religious exercise or this or that belief system will serve instead is naïve to say the least. We exist in an order we didn't create via the light energy of love we did not create and the only way to live well in that order is to live in harmony with it.

There are those who claim this or that sacrifice will please the Intelligence. The bigger the gift the more it should please Him or Her! But it was the Intelligence who made it all in the first place. It "owns" it all. To give the Deity what it already has is only a human unrealistic and illogical concoction. Our Heavenly Father wants us to be a part of what is good for us and what will sustain the harmony already built into this creation He made via the means He has made.

Living pleasantly!

If our Creator's goal for us is only to live pleasantly, then this creation is a vast mistake. We don't, we can't, live up to that kind of potential in our given circumstances. We have attitudes and mind sets which prevent it and we seldom have the desire and the persistence to correct our aberrant behavior even with divine help. By commission and omission we are less than what we should be. Every other entity in this creation obeys Natural Law. All of us, to some degree, know the choices and we too often choose what contributes to chaos.

Maybe the Intelligence couldn't figure this out before we were given the ability to know something of right and wrong and what we would do with that choice! Ignorance in the All-knowing? Preposterous!

But what if the Intelligence had enough sense to know that if He or She gave us the right of choice, that we would sometimes, even persistently, choose badly? Were we created as we are so that we could then be punished? Is the Deity a sadist? Again, preposterous!

The hand of love

We see the hand of the Intelligence all about us, caring for this creation, meeting its fundamental needs, respecting each individual species so they have a niche in the larger picture and understanding the whole of this intricate reality, the definition of love given us by Dr. Fromm in "The Art of Loving." This creation is good and its harmonies are good—we humans are the problem. We know differently from what we sometimes do. We know from childhood the obedience/cookies routine, and we still create the problems. So why do we exist? Why were we placed, why was each of us placed, in this Natural Law world, with its Zero Point Field?

This will be the focus of Chapter Four, the Role of the Spirit that is Holy. Sufficient to say that when we can begin to understand something of the grand purpose of it all, the intelligence and love of the One can be no better illustrated than how this impasse is resolved. For the moment let us turn to the existence and the role of the Zero Point Field in the Creator's Plan which facilitates our potential for living well.

A Meditation

Why is it so difficult for us, for me, Heavenly Father
      To accept the realities of Natural Law?
It is evident in every aspect of this Creation around me
      From the tectonic plates and the visiting comets
            To the minutest of the entities in the Zero Point Field.
They are, I am and I can exist well
      Only if I live in harmony with it all
I too often live day by day, year by year
      Numbed to the realities of my very existence
I too often try to justify my ignoring it
      As though it is no great matter
When every blockage of Your love light energy
      Affects the energy field in me
And the dimensions of my energy field affects
      All energy fields about me
I sense an influence within me which would block
      My involvement in being part of Your Will

Every moment lived in some diversion
    Any time spent removed from my spiritual umbilical cord
        Weakens the life force within me
        And the flowage of that life-force about me
I can live passively, non-assertively,
    And live on the leftovers of life
But I choose to involve myself with the essence of life
    To take away any sin blockage of Your energy flow
        The light energy flowage available for me through love
I choose to walk with You in the spirit and in truth
    In every Existential Now of my living
I commit to striving to recognize the order of Natural Law
    And the ongoing means You have created
        To sustain this order
        Through Your omnipotent, omnipresent and omniscient Will
Your Way of Life through love
    Will become my way of Life through love
As I follow You, my Blessed Shepherd, into the green pastures
    And still waters of life.

CHAPTER THREE

The Spiritual Dynamic: The Zero Point Field

We have looked at the magnificence of Natural Law, its order, its universality and its harmony—one set of laws for all time. Its evidence in nature is available any time we seek it. It is in the life and teachings of Jesus any time we take the time to listen. It is such a privilege to go out into the natural world, into a garden, and just allow the order, the beautiful harmony, to flow into one's soul. Life is so rich when we allow the harmony and symmetry of the Sustaining Will through Natural Law to flow into us.

Through science we have come to understand those laws. We know more about our environment than any other people in all human history. Through the computer this knowledge is at our fingertips. But is that all? After we have satisfied our need for food, shelter and clothing, built our technological societies, what is left for us, for me, to do, to be? What is life all about anyway?

We cannot avoid those "why" questions! Why am I here? Why me? What is expected of me? After I have more or less met my needs for taking care of my body, and there is part of me which is never totally satisfied, I am becoming aware of so much more! In the quiet moments, sometimes in the night, perhaps when I am out in nature or in my garden, I am aware of something, some connectedness, some part of me that yearns for a dimension of life that is satisfied only by spiritual things.

My parents weren't church goers. As a teen-ager I attended a confirmation class which touched me deeply. I became aware of so much. It was as if I found something that satisfied my deepest yearnings. After seventy years it is still there, this special connectedness to something far more than satisfying than the needs of my body.

As I was reading my Bible one day, back again in those teen years, I ran across the story of Solomon, how God asked what gift he would like to be given. (I Kings 3:5-9) The Lord was pleased when Solomon wanted knowledge. That touched me and became my prayer. I have spent a life time as a scholar and researcher.

The Lord has been a wonderful Shepherd for this farm boy, guiding me into the best of scholarly studies, the best of schools and the opportunities as a teacher to learn from teaching—there is no better format for that! What a gift to read the writings of those who led the early church! What a gift to study church history, both its failures and its achievements! What a gift to study philosophy and theology, what the best of minds have understood about spiritual matters down through the ages! What a gift are the Fine Arts! That Fifth Commandment about honoring our spiritual parentage has come home to me so often. Through it all my Good Shepherd has led me to so many green pastures and waters of rest. (Psalm 23:1&2)

The Spirit that is Holy has given us the gifts to not only understand Natural Law, but the why of it. We discover we have the gifts to answer these questions about this world in which we find ourselves. Man the tool-maker allows us to survive in this world. Man the symbol-maker tackles the questions of Who and why!

Man the symbol user

We instinctively turn to symbols, physical objects and words with spiritual connotations, when we think and talk about the spiritual world. We shall need the best of our skills of the use of the symbolic when we address the Who and the why, for they remain largely unseen to our physical eye sight. That is difficult for us, more difficult for some people than for others. Symbols allow us to interact with the unseen world by using physical imagery from which to derive spiritual meanings, as in the Fine Arts.

A word of caution here. The unseen does not exist nor have its existence because of our belief or disbelief in it. It is whatever it is and we are what we are. It is in our best moments that we tackle the questions concerning our existence for we have that within us which must make sense out of our own existence. Again, I am, but what and why am I?

Although some would deny this, there is no human who does not overtly or covertly have to deal with the issue of the spiritual world. It is easy to deny it all, but why? Why not engage the beauty and the order, the symmetry and the harmony of life within and about us? Again, we are so much more than atoms and molecules!

Certainly there is the ugly and the destructive. But is that all? To allow it to be the all of our living, to not open to the beauty and the joy of life, is to insist on chewing on stale crackers when a feast is offered us, to short-change our very living. To care for our body and not for our soul is tunnel vision personified. And the wider vistas are there for anyone who will lift up their eyes above the muck and the mire and allow the beauty of the Creator to enter into their troubled souls. To open to the love of our Heavenly Father, to open to the spiritual dimension of life, is to find life which is life indeed.

Jesus stated it bluntly, it is the spirit that gives life, the flesh profits nothing! (John 6:63) As one studies the teachings and the ministry of Jesus we discover that it is one long attempt to lift us up from the purely physical and engage and develop a spiritual dimension, a wider perspective, in our lives.

Here everyone must face one of the basic realities of human living. One day we shall lay aside our physical bodies and journey as a spiritual entity into the Spiritual World. This is reality. Hadn't we better be prepared for that journey?

Jesus spoke a great truth in the quotation above: it is our spirit that gives life, the flesh profits nothing. Our physical entity will follow the laws of entropy and eventually die. But if we attend to our spiritual entity, it will grow and develop into a being capable of dwelling in the Spiritual World. One decreases, the other is designed to increase, if we walk the Way of Life through love outlined by Jesus. Our time in our physical bodies could be described as one long struggle to allow our spiritual entity to grow and develop so we can inhabit eternity: the mustard seed described by Jesus. (Matthew 13:31, 32)

The spiritual revelations of God are available in the law and order of the Natural Law expressed in the Ten Commandments, in the life and teachings of Jesus and through the work of the indwelling Holy Spirit which we sometimes call our conscience. Too many people will be so preoccupied with the physical that they will not even hear the Word. Some will hear and respond, but under criticism they will give it up. Others will respond but the desires of the physical will crowd out and destroy spiritual growth. Still others will respond and allow the spiritual dimension of their lives to develop and grow, some more than others. (Matthew 13:1-12, 18-23)

This spiritual development, if allowed to happen, will take place in the midst of those who don't open to the ways of the Spirit, as in the Parable of the Tares (weeds). (Matthew 13:24-30, 37-43) A table is prepared for us in the presence of those who trouble us. (Psalm 23:5)

It is a matter of priorities: we will either seek the physical and attempt to satisfy ourselves with the physical or we will allow the spiritual to grow in our lives. One or the other will prevail. One leads to life after life and the other to a span of existence in the physical body and that is it! Those who so choose miss the ultimate reason for their existence!

The focus on the Spirit in the Bible is evident. It is mentioned two hundred and fifty-six times! Nicodemus was told that he had to have a spiritual citizenship or his religious life was useless. (John 3:1-6) "That which is born of the flesh is flesh and that which is of the spirit is spirit." The Samaritan Woman was told we are to worship God in the spirit and in truth. (John 4:23, 24) "God is spiritual, and they who worship Him must worship in the Spirit and in truth, for such the Father seeks to worship Him."

God's Plan of salvation is simply stated in Attachment One of this work. Briefly, God has provided humans the mental ability and the spiritual hunger to seek Him in the Spirit, and to allow our spiritual connectedness to grow until, when we lay aside our physical nature, we are able to journey into the Spiritual World and live there.

As stated above, man the tool-maker has allowed us to dominate this earth physically, but unless we become man the symbol-maker, and allow that symbol-making process to lead us into a love-bond with our Creator and Redeemer, we have missed the reason for our existence!

Symbol making

Just as physical tools allow us to find food, shelter and clothing, so the tools we use to penetrate the unseen about us are symbols, be they language imagery, visual and material objects or auditory sounds. Symbols are tangible entities that have a larger meaning, something seen that evokes the unseen. A flag may evoke patriotism, a beautiful figure may evoke emotions of desire, a poem may evoke a vision of beauty, likewise music and the rest of the arts. We have surrounded ourselves with symbolic experiences that evoke various emotions, sometimes very strong reactions, sometime very little and sometimes rejections. Reactions to symbols are very personal. The Fine Arts are symbolic expressions in various media.

Then we get to the world of religion. Since the Deity and all the other experiences we have with the unseen spiritual world are almost by definition unseen, we must rely on symbols to try to make sense of our spiritual encounters. Here is where the trouble begins. As one art work may excite someone and another have no reaction to it, as it is with music, poetry, etc., so it is with religion! One can say without exaggeration that everyone has a different view and understanding of the spiritual dimension of their lives, varying from total rejection to fanatic fixation.

So the great "why" questions of our lives inevitably lead us into field which we usually call "religion." We have a long history here.

Religions of human history

Many millenniums ago mankind apparently gathered in caves in France to paint pictures of mostly animals but some humans as well; pictures which can still be witnessed today, where, in flickering torch light the animal figures take on a vibrant life. Evidence of ritual procedures remain to this day.

Excavations in Jericho at the earliest level, sometimes dated to many thousands of years B.C.E., reveal a temple shaped like a woman's womb. Egyptian tombs reveal elaborate preparations for the dead person's afterlife. Temples, burial sites, decoded early cuneiform and Egyptian writings, speak of gods and goddesses, their rituals and worship procedures. Religious persecutions and wars over which deity is the right deity proliferate in human history. The earliest religions seem to be based on attempts to please a deity on the premise that pleasing resulted in blessings.

A religion with a moral base

The Bible records the giant step forward when religious behavior was changed from pleasing a deity to recognizing the fact that this world is based upon moral laws, which we have labeled Natural Law, and living in accord with those laws would please the Creator of this world. A brief version of the rules upon which this creation operated, the Ten Commandments, was given to us because of the love of the Creator for us! To live morally is to live well in this world in which we find ourselves!

Commandment One and Two of the Ten Commandments: there is only one Deity and therefore only one system of Natural Law in this world; don't provide a human substitute! Historically priesthoods have resisted this step for it takes away from them their privileged state. Ideally they were to function as a facilitator of the one system. What too often happened is a reflection of man's earliest sin—they wanted to make the rules and benefit from those who came to worship in their temples by those rules! This struggle existed throughout the Biblical writings. It was the priesthood that killed Jesus.

The "how" basis of moral laws

So, in our better moments, we have come to realize that we need to obey the Natural Law to please our Deity and that was for our own good. But is that all? Jesus gave us another new perspective—we are to love the things of Jesus, learn how to love as the basis of our ethical behavior which would then develop into a love-bond and develop a friendship relationship with Jesus. (John 21:15-17) We can accept the gift of Jesus' death for our salvation and then commit to learning how to live out this special relationship, the Gospel Covenant, in a love-based ethic founded upon Natural Law.

But the question remains, beyond our faith, who and what is this Deity who created and sustains this creation of His? What does He or She want of us, of me? This has been food for the philosophers, the theologians and lately the psychologists, down through the ages. How does the spiritual fit in with the physical?

The Jesus revelation

Jesus' answer to our questions was outlined at the end of the last chapter. God's revelation, expressed in the Bible as part of the order of Natural Law, is contained in the life and teachings of Jesus and personally expressed through the inner voice of our indwelling Holy Spirit. These revelations work. The Gospel Covenant facilitates life and will lead us to the promised "green pastures and still waters." But that has not stopped humans from creating supposed answers, all human Towers of Babel.

The problem we face in religious thinking

The problem was and continues to be the unseen nature of spiritual entities. Any gifted speaker or story teller can concoct a "revelation" of how it is. But do these "insights" correspond to Natural Law, the love ethic of Jesus and the inner voice of peace, love and joy of the Holy Spirit, who always speaks in consort with Natural Law and the love basis of Jesus—the Holy Trinity? Where is the physical scientific proof of who and what God is and wants of us?

Hume's Proposition

The philosopher David Hume stated the problem well: That which can not be quantified can not be qualified by scientific procedure and analysis. What cannot be weighed and measured by physical means: scales, yard sticks, etc., can not be proved to exist by scientific, empirical analysis. Scientific procedures depend upon physical evidence for the formulas and the procedures it uses in order to establish facts.

The howls of protest from religious leaders reverberated throughout the religious world. Hume had simply stated the reality that physical measurements of physical entities cannot be used to establish the truth of a spiritual entity! How could they?

Kirkegaard and existentialism

So the matter stood for more than half a century until Soren Kirkegaard stated the matter in another simple formula: Spiritual entities cannot be "measured" by physical means but the human results of what they are and teach can certainly be evaluated! What kind of societies, what kind of individuals are produced by adherence to a given religious idea? The proof of the pudding is in the eating!

How long will it take for spiritual people to raise the outcry over the horrendous results of religions such as Islam, Socialism and

Communism? Their physical results prove the falsity of these Towers of Babel!

The role of science

There is nothing evil about science. Scientific methods and procedures are but means to be used in human pursuits of truth. Through the scientific process we have learned and recorded thick volumes of the laws by which atoms are organized into useful molecules. We have learned to assemble them into the tools necessary for our existence. We have the periodic table of chemistry, the laws of physics, the seeming order of sociology and economics and the human understandings of psychology, etc.

But to assume that the systems of atoms and molecules we learned over the last four hundred years is all there is, is naïve indeed. The curiosity that impelled the great strides in learning did not end at the beginning of the twentieth century!

Emerging Quantum mechanics

By the nineteen twenties cracks began to appear in the smooth certainties of Newtonian physics. Physicists, including Einstein, recognized that there exists a field of energy which surrounds and undergirds life, giving incredible diverse character to the simple atomic structures we recognized. The study of quantum mechanics came into being. Fields of energy exists in all living matter, in every living cell. It is of particular significance to human beings because of our mental/spiritual capabilities.

Sigmund Freud

In quite another arena, psychiatrists such as Sigmund Freud were exploring the human unconscious. Our human consciousness seems to be but the tip of an iceberg, nine-tenths of it submerged in a mystic unknown yet having a profound influence upon human choice capabilities.

Freud exhibits the narrowness of too many of the research individuals. According to him, religion needed to be seen as outmoded and a thing of the human past; all is to be understood via the human sex drive. But his ideas of the human ego being involved in a conflict between the destructive and antisocial Id and the socially acceptable and workable Super Ego was but a rehash of a long ago religion of Zoroastrianism. Substitute Ahura Mazda for the Super Ego and Ania Meinyu for the Id and one has the ancient struggle between the light and the darkness, the good and the bad and the cults that have formed through different language terms used for the same phenomena. The struggle is real but the terms and the meaning of it all is best communicated by the One who came from Heaven to Earth to tell us all about it and how to make it work in human lives and affairs.

Carl Jung

Carl Jung used a somewhat different set of language terms in his approach to the unconscious part of human cognition. His interests and studies in psychiatry, particularly of the unconscious, led to studies in the same arena as the Zero Point Field. His monumental work in the power of myths, archetypes and the tribal unconscious are giant steps into the same area as was being explored by the scientists attempting to understand the vast subconscious of human existence. Sadly, Jung rejected the role of Jesus in this matter, which makes his work scattered but brilliant, penetrating but without the central spiritual core. For further studies in this dimension of human cognition, "The Portable Jung," edited by Joseph Campbell, is an excellent source.

We shall probably never know anything like all there is to know about this field. As we shall see, so much of our knowledge is tied to our attitudes and mind sets of our larger living. But the beginnings of quantum mechanics were made when it was realized that simple Newtonian physics couldn't answer many questions. It began with light itself, its peculiar behavior and the fact that humans could influence something of the peculiar behavior of light. Light is sometimes beams and sometimes waves and one could not predict when it would be which! Yet it could be influenced by human will! Amazing!

The Zero Point Field (ZPF)

Years of research in the finest of research institutions have revealed an invisible field of existence that is all inclusive, uniting and is part of every cell. It is called the Zero Point Field because it continues its activities when temperatures reach absolute zero, that is, it doesn't seem to be influenced by temperature. It isn't a particle field, although it influences particles. It is an invisible field not influenced by gravity. As indicated earlier, Lynne McTaggert's book, "The Field," is an excellent introduction to the research done in this arena of study.

Why should we concern ourselves with this phenomenon? A key issue is the influence of human will on our brain, our attitudes and our ability to purvey information. Scientific tests have proven what we have long known, that we can influence molecular structures without boundaries as to distance. The key is the love bond. Couples in a love-bond relationship "know" what another is thinking or feeling without being in direct contact with them. At times we can experience an event in another's life though separated by space and even time. Once one allows these dimensions of knowledge to develop one can even know what is going on in another place! Most people simply debunk such ideas but that very debunking means they have ruled themselves out of being able to understand its potential. Willful ignorance never enhanced knowledge!

Human unity through the Zero Point Field

It is through the Zero Point Field that all humans are united in all time. It is Jung's Tribal Unconscious using a different language. We share this field. For most people this is irrelevant but the reality of its existence should never be discounted, for it has a direct impact on our living.

To the observant—life is all about and within us. Life consists of energy fields. Every living energy field exists in cycles, each having a beginning, a growing, an aging and an ending so new cycles can begin. For that matter all entities, even mountains, tectonic plates and stellar entities have their cycles of existence. All are part of energy fields adjacent and influencing one another within an all encompassing field—all related to each other in every moment of our life's experiences. We have the maxim, "I am I and you are you, and we are all each other too."

It is significant that we recognize the interacting and interdependent cycles of all living entities. Animals and plants cannot ask the "why" and the "therefore" of this interconnection but we humans were given frontal lobe abilities to derive meanings for our existence from this phenomenon. The quality of our life is dependent upon how we handle our moment by moment experiences of the interconnectedness of our living through this Zero Point Field.

The Mozart Effect

Every living entity has its own energy field. We have instruments, such as Fritz-Albert's photonmultiplier, which can measure the energy fields of living matter. Trees have their fields, each having a song. The songs have sometimes been called the "Mozart Effect" because their songs come close to the compositions of Mozart. For a report on some of the research done on this matter one can read "The Mozart Effect," by Dan Campbell.

Too many people have chosen to live in a mechanical world of predictable atoms and molecules. The idea of a uniting and all encompassing energy field which is invisible and cannot be totally understood by Newtonian physics is frightening to many. The simple known is safe, orderly and comfortable. It won't lead into spiritual possibilities! But it is chewing on dry crackers when our Creator has placed a banquet within this creation. Life can be rich and full and beautiful, why settle on the mundane and the colorless, why not explore the unknown wherever it may lead?

Physical light

Physical light makes life possible in our world. Photosynthesis is essential for plants. We respond to light and darkness, both psychologically and physically. Light is energy—love energy from the sustaining Source. There is a continual struggle in any living entity between growing through that light energy by receiving that energy and its fading, allowing the laws of entropy to take over. Entropy, the dispersion of concentrations of energy, is part of this creation. When a living being loses its energy field, its ability to function via light energy, it is dead. It has completed its cycle of existence.

Our earth and all its inhabitants have been given light energy and therefore life. It is the energy from the Source that sustains this creation. By mathematical calculations more than eighty percent of our cosmos consists of invisible matter. As stated earlier, we know of its existence because gravity alone cannot keep the various comets, planets, stars and galaxies together and in their orbits.

The Will of the Absolute

Concentrations of human will can influence matter, as proven in the quantum physics research listed in McTaggert's book. If human will can and does influence matter, why cannot an Absolute Will do so? At present we cannot physically measure the influence of human will. We know it exists by observation. The Absolute Will, although invisible, maintains and sustains the order of this world. It works; it is functioning!

It is so important that we maintain an objective attitude on matters of exploring new fields of existence. Bias, prejudices, "it can't be" attitudes, simply put blinders on observations. The Zero Point Field exists. It is a light energy flow. It influences all matter and controls all matter. This is reality.

It is so important that we reach beyond human philosophies and theologies, even psychological explanations without the spiritual, when we try to come to terms with what science has opened up for us. It is time to lay aside human explanations and theories and rely on the facts of Natural Law in this field of invisible light energy.

The Biblical references

This is expressed in the first verses of the Bible! Creation began with light. As indicated above, this life is lived in cycles of birth/beginning, growing, aging and ending. All existence has only the reality of the present moment, which we label the Existential Now. At this moment we are immersed in life, from the solar light to the energy flow in all that is living about us and within us. At this moment every living entity is somewhere in the cycles of their life, immersed in the Will of the Creator. Our human problem is that we can receive only as much of that Will as can get through the personal obstructions we place as obstacles through our attitudes and belief systems.

Human obstacles to the Will

Only humans have the capability of personally forestalling and blocking that steam of energy emanating from the Source. Through our attitudes, mind sets, amoral behavior and prejudices we can block the energy stream of light/love from influencing our consciousness. Behavior inconsistent with the order of Natural Law, moral rebellion, which we have labeled evil, or sin, can block the pervading Will from entering or directing our person. We cannot do anything to the Will, but we can close that Will to its influences on our personal behavior. The awesome power of humans!

The natural world remains in harmony with the purposes of its existence. We humans have not, through our own choices. Because of the influence of others, the personality problems within us, and the behavioral choices we make, we are not anything like what we are capable of becoming.

Living our life in cyclical time

We will live out our life in cycles. Whether short or long, each cycle is designed to be part of our Creator's Plan for the human race: which is spiritual growth that will allow us to live in harmony with the Will after we lay aside our physical bodies. We can learn how to be open to the sustaining Will every moment of our living. We live in cycles designed to expedite that growth. Every cycle ends so a new cycle can begin. It is the resurrection power which Jesus spoke of when He said He was resurrection and life. (John 11:25) New beginnings, the ability to lay aside the old and begin anew, is central to our spiritual development.

We have the energy from the Source to make that growth possible. It all depends upon whether we will learn from our existential experiences what to lay aside and what to take into our belief system so we can fulfill the Plan for our personal existence; which is spiritual growth into something of our potential in love, joy, peace, patience, kindness, goodness, faithfulness, gentleness and self-discipline. That is the work of the Spirit that is Holy in our lives.

We will not be perfect, but those very problems, failures and wrong turns are to be used by the individual as learning steps into wholeness—holiness. We humans have the great gift of learning. We can redo the tapes that govern our actions. We can reject the lesser and take on the greater, using the cycles of our living as stepping stones to absorbing greater and larger amounts of the love energy of life from the Source. We can learn what doesn't work and not repeat it. We can learn what does work and build upon it. But it must all be done based on the reality of the natural laws which govern this Creation. We need to commit to allowing the love/light energy flow from the Source, the One, into our lives if we would live well in this creation in which we find ourselves.

Living in a moral universe

By this standard we live in a moral creation. Certain behaviors are in harmony with that system and certain ones are not. We cannot escape the simple dilemma to live well is to live in harmony with the laws; to live well is to allow the light energy of life to flow unimpeded into our being.

Virtual realities

We humans, by our imaginations, have created many forms of virtual reality. Indeed every action we make is based upon our version of how-it-is, a personal or imposed form of virtual reality. We have lived in our versions of reality so long that we sometimes assume they are real! The key to mental health is recognizing the degree of reality in our constructs of virtual realities!

We live together in cities, in artificial human creations of buildings, means of conveyance, eating habits and clothing with its attendant emersion in noise created by human instruments of communication and technology. In doing so, we have largely lost vital connections with reality, of the harmonies possible by being in sync with Natural Law as sustained by the Will. Most people could not survive in the natural world! We live out our lives in a sea of virtual realities! But is that all there is? How could it be? How could a just and loving Creator not offer us something better?

Worse than that, we have too often lost a desire to be a part of Natural Law when our virtual realities provide easier and more pleasurable diversions. We surround ourselves with educational formats, political formats, physical wishes and human ideas of how-it-is derived from psychology, economics and sociology. All are available from merchants who make their living servicing us with those baubles! As a result we find the natural world distasteful and even dangerous. It becomes a continual temptation to live in a continuum of chosen or imposed virtual realities; by definition an "unsane" world!

But does this estrangement change Natural Law? Does it change the light-love energy from the Source? Does it change the Zero Point Field? Of course not! How could it?

The Natural World continues to exist, hurt, misunderstood, destroyed by many through ignorance and design, but long after the last human will have died it will retain its harmonic structure and continue on as it did for the billions of years before humans arrived.

Ditto the Will of the Source. But, since this creation exists to produce spiritual entities capable of living in the Spiritual World, when it no longer does so it will be destroyed making room for a New Heaven and a New Earth which has never been sullied by sin; to be inhabited by spiritual entities who will not destroy it through their sin!

Time

The reality is that not only is our world run upon Natural Law and sustained by the Will through the Zero Point Field, but the entities of this world, both living and non-living, exist in cycles of what we call time. Time is a measurement of the cycles of life. The cycles exist but human names for them vary by the cultures. We use the designations of day, week, month, etc. But within the Zero Point Field there is only existence or non-existence. Therefore human time as related to the Zero Point Field has no meaning except as we impose our time designations. 20 B.C.E, today and 2200 are all part of the same existence within the Zero Point Field. How else could it be?

Is the Zero Point Field eternal? No, is is part of this creation. It is part of the larger cycle of beginning the Plan of God, developing and aging that Plan through the Sustaining Will and the planned ending so that a new beginning with a New Heaven and a New Earth untainted by human sin becomes possible.

All living and non-living entities have a cycle of life within the larger and overarching cycle. Each cycle is fed by the light energy of love connected through the Zero Point Field. Each energy field of life has its own song, its own action within the larger symphony. Every cycle has its teleological purpose, its reason for existence, its role in the larger patterns of existence.

This is no longer just a matter of faith based upon the Jesus Message. As mentioned above, we have instruments which can measure this energy field and the impact upon that field by humanly constructed virtual realities such as those spun by hate, anger, jealousy, envy, covetousness and lust. Human creations of virtual reality are transitory. They come and go with the advent and demise of every human and every human assemblage. The only ultimate reality is the real thing existing in the Source!

Laying aside the hindrances

It is essential for our living for us to lay aside every diversion of virtual human creations of realities and regain a personal and interactive relationship of love and care with the One, the Order-maker, if we would live well. Light is real. Life is real. Love is real. The energy flow of life through the light of love is real. It impacts every human whether we wish it to or not. And there is the rub!

Every human is born into this world which is run by the precepts of Natural Law and sustained by the Will united and expedited through the Zero Point Energy Field. We are also part of the energy fields of all entities both living and non-living about us, for the dividing line between living and non-living is not absolute in reality—all are part of a larger continuum of life sometimes referred to as the Gaia principle.

The Gaia Principle

This principle, mentioned earlier, is this creation's ability to right itself after injury; to heal wounds, to return to the original equilibrium of its existence. In this sense, as referred to above, the Stoics had it partly right. Nature has a force, an existence, a system of life. The big mistake of the Stoics was to assume nature exercised this order by its own power. We know that nature, based as it is upon Natural Law, is but an expression of the Intelligence that organized what we call nature. Life is in the sustaining power of the Will of the One which makes possible all existence and order.

Our human response

Every human will responds to this existence in their own way. We are part of this universal principle whether we wish it to be so or not. We can always opt out of this existence by overt or covert suicide. But we can also accept it as a reality and learn to live splendidly by its precepts. We have been given the ultimate quality of the light/ energy force, the key to the operation of the Zero Point Field in our living—love.

Love

There is a basic component to the light/energy field—the emotion we call love. I will use the definition of love provided by Dr. Fromm in his work, "The Art of Love," mentioned above. Love is that which cares, which responds to need, which respects the individual and which leads to understandings based upon the realities of Natural Law and the Will of the Source.

Love cares by extending itself for the spiritual welfare of another. It is willing to expend one's time, energy and possessions for the pleasure derived by sharing, by the joy that caring gives the giver, for the spiritual welfare it provides the receiver.

Acts of love are given in response to real need. It is easy to just say "need," but there are times when giving to false needs actually injure the receiver. Giving that cements the receiver further into a dependent relationship is not a love sharing. Gifts of love help the receiver to deal with real issues in a manner that facilitates their spiritual development. Love is designed to build love. We give in the name of Jesus that the recipient may build a relationship with Jesus through the gift.

Love always respects the individual, the person, of the receiver. Every human is unique. True love always builds upon the specialness of the receiver.

Love attempts to understand the situation that exists in the existential moments of the relationship. It is an extension of the "I am I and you are you and we are both each other too." It is the "each other also" that builds special moments of understanding and sharing that can be mountain top experiences.

The human emotion of love is an essential part of the light/life energy which is designed to under gird and make possible in human consciousnesses the realization of God's Plan through His Will using the channel of the Zero Point Field. Love is essential for human life and living. Infants literally die for lack of it. All human activity and personal developments are warped for lack of it. The power center, the Sustainer discussed above, is the personification of love. (I John 4:8)

In the Quantum Mechanics world, energy equals life and it is love which facilitates the light/energy channels. In all the experiments of giving and receiving by means of the Zero Point Field, where there was a love bond the energy flow was always greatly facilitated. Every human relationship is strengthened over time via the development of a love bond which facilitates the giving and the sharing until it becomes an awareness that needs no words and is not bound by space or time. Where there is light there is life and that life is sustained by caring, responsive, respecting and understanding love as it works its invisible energy upon our spiritual essence. God is love and that which is part of love is part of the Sustainer's Will.

The Lie

There exists also a false light, a lie, a pseudo-illumination which leads to destructiveness and death. An essential part of that syndrome is hate and fear. That is why wars are so destructive—love disappears as hate and fear dominate the world! There is a reason why Jesus said, "Blessed are the peace-makers for they shall be called the children of God." (Matthew 5:9) In the fury of hate and murder the light from the Source is undiminished but it is obscured by human destructiveness. We humans have the awesome capability of warping our perception and therefore the reception of the love light! It is as Jesus said, "The lamp of the body is the eye. If the eye is healthy, the whole body is full of light. If the eye is unhealthy, the body will be full of darkness. If the light that is within us is darkness, how great is that darkness!' (Matthew 6:22, 23) God could not give us the ability to give and receive love without the possibility blocking and destroying this elixir of life for ourselves and others. That is an awesome capability we have been given!

That which leads to the destructiveness, the chaos, the downward slide from fixation to obsession to possession is always based upon fear leading to hate. The agents of this anti-order have been allowed into this creation by its Creator. Why? For our spiritual development!

The why of struggles

It is a reality that it is through our struggles that we discover our need for a savior. God the Provider has provided a way of salvation in Jesus, who is an expression of the sustaining light of love through the Will from the Source. We must recognize our need for this Savior before we will repent of the behavior patterns that got us into our situations and commit to a change. We will not change as long as we think the old is working!

The Five R's of Repentance

The way of repentance is by way of the Five R's of repentance: Recognizing the sin, Repenting, saying we are sorry, Rejecting the behavior that got us into the mess, Remembering our Higher Power for the necessary strength to make the change and then Rebuilding our lives in a new and better way. Without our struggles we would float along through life in some virtual reality, some deviant thinking, some form of nothingness!

Temptations with virtual notions that don't work have allowed us to recognize the reality of agents of evil, which in our language, we have labeled devils. They are spiritual entities who have chosen to make a world of their own run by their order and through coercion. They are allowed into our world so we who follow Jesus will have to choose that which works at whatever the cost again and again in the face of temptations. It is by those choices in our struggles to live via the love energy of light that we develop into creatures who can live in the New Heaven and the New Earth. After cycles of spiritual warfare, choosing the morally right in harmony with the Will, because we love and want those harmonies, that we can be depended upon to not become seduced and therefore corrupt the new world God will create when this old one has no longer served its purpose. This is all part of God's Plan—to produce spiritual beings who have come out of this life as committed followers of the Jesus Way of Life through love.

We experience the presence of such negative power centers. Opening to the temptations of this anti-order, based upon fear and hate, always depletes and shrinks our receptions from the Source and therefore our energy fields. As this shrinkage affects all energy fields associated with us, so our removal by God's strength of the blockages to the Sustainer's light energy of love flowage, builds a spiritual strength within us and spreads the light of God around us. We become, through allowing the Zero Point Field's energy of love to flow through us, the light of the world. (Matthew 5:14-16)

The foundation principle, the sustaining force of this creation is light energy based upon love exercised through the Zero Point Field. All of life, the physical visible creation, as well as the invisible to the physical eye, is alive, vibrant with life or it is a living black hole. If it is in harmony with the Orderer, it is beautiful to the spiritual eye tuned to that order, the harmony and the symmetry of Natural Law. There are, however, enticing black holes of nothingness, into which evil attempts to allure us. It is all part of our associations with the Zero Point Field existing within each of us. Pleasant or not, this is existential reality. We are either learning to be in harmony with this light/love energy flow or we are choosing a virtual reality which does not work in this creation. Some choose to live in open rebellion, while others in passive-aggressive resistance. But the Jesus Way of Life is an ark type reality. We are either in the ark or we aren't!

Our individual spark of light and love energy

Each individual has the spark of this light/life/love syndrome within them. We are so much more than a machine. We are an existential being in need of the light/love energy for our living. We need the foundation of love and commitment to righteousness which makes that living possible. It all depends upon our willingness to be agents of that love in our daily living. We choose and by our choices we allow our spiritual essences to develop into something of its potential. That is the topic of the next chapter—the spiritual entity, which for conversational purposes we have labeled the Holy Spirit, by which we finite beings can learn how to live well in this vast infinity of existence during our brief cycle of existence.

Human virtual realities

It is so easy for us, with our gift of imagination, to use our gift of language to construct some human system of virtual reality. Facing life and the realities of our living is not always pleasant. There is that which entices us into behavior which is not part of the harmony built upon Natural Law. No dependence upon positive thinking alone will annihilate that negative power in our lives. Evil can only be replaced by acts of love based upon attitudes of love in harmony with the light of life from the Source.

This struggle between the charade, the mirage, the false will be with us throughout our living. The Spirit that is Holy was sent to indwell our inner being so we would have a light to guide and empower us for spiritual living. But that Spirit will not be heard unless we take time to be in such a manner that He can be heard. That is the reason for that Fourth Commandment: "Remember the Sabbath Day and keep it holy." Satan will do everything possible to keep us so occupied that we will not take time out to be in contact with God.

The goodness of our Lord's Way

God's Will is goodness personified. We are to live positively in harmony with it. The very light energy from the Source is positive. Our focus is to be on the positive.

Evil will attempt to get us to focus on the negative, what is wrong with the world we live in. And there is plenty of that! However, to face the negative reality under the guise of "see no evil, hear no evil, speak no evil and there is no evil" is ostrich in the sand mentality. Recognizing evil and dwelling upon it are two different things. We shall explore this further in the next chapter.

It is too easy to regard the light, love, life syndrome as pleasant philosophy and it is that, but it is so much more. It is life. It is the first verses of the Bible. It is life reaching out to every human through the Zero Point Field of every cell of our makeup through love in action. Well could Paul write that even if we speak wisdom, can move mountains with prayer and give our bodies as sacrifices, without love we are nothing. (I Corinthians 13:1f)

This universe is one magnificent energy field expressing the goodness and the love of the Intelligence which made it. Every entity, every living, as well as the non-living part of this energy field, is part of one grand unity of which every human is invited to play a part. We are so much more than a machine. We are designed to be an expression of love, beauty, joy and goodness in harmony with the all encompassing Will of our Creator through our personal associations flowing through our contact with the Zero Point Field.

The Intelligence has provided a way for us to become an expression, each a special individual expression of the Divine Goodness. Each existential moment is an invitation to share in the goodness, the beauty, the special amalgamation of entities into a unity of diversity, the ultimate family of God. All are part of the Plan of God executed in day by day expressions of His Will. We can choose to be part of this glorious assemblage or reject it in favor of our own constructs of nothingness!

Before Jesus returned to Heaven He told His followers to wait in Jerusalem for the coming of the Spirit that is Holy. On that first Pentecost, the Jewish holiday of thanksgiving, they experienced the phenomenon that now embraces every human—the indwelling of the divine which we call the Holy Spirit. It resides in the unconscious of every human. It arises into our consciousness in what we have termed our "conscience."

Through the silent voice of persuasion and love it attempts to guide us into the truth of Natural Law based upon the love foundation by Jesus expressed through the overarching Will through the Zero Point Field. It ever seeks to draw us into a unity of love based beauty, of goodness personified in acts of love, of truth multiplied by love in action. It is a way in which the valleys of life become part of the road of life, the struggles become moments of enlightenment and the darkness becomes a background for the light of life itself. Let us turn to the work of the Holy Spirit.

A Meditation

How can I ever thank You enough, Heavenly Father
    Lord Jesus, Holy Spirit, Holy Angels
        For this plan of salvation You have prepared for me
You created a world which testifies of Your truth in Natural Law
    You built into this world
        Into every living cell of this world
    The light energy field of love
        Needed to sustain this world
            Needed to sustain my spiritual growth and development
All I have to do is allow it to happen
    Quit putting up the barriers
        That keep You from cleansing the old
        And resurrecting new life in me
Father, I am but a humble human child
    Hungry for Your love and joy and peace
I want what You have to offer
    I want to live in greater harmony with the order of Natural Law
    I want to take down the barriers to Your Will
By Your grace and strength I wish to rid myself
    Of attitudes, mind sets, learning that is not learning
        Virtual realities that are not reality
Whatever it takes, however I need to go
    I would walk it by Your grace
I would have this spark of divinity
    Which You have placed within me
Be able to develop and grow through Your Grace and strength
    As my physical entity fades in the entropy of life's cycle
For I want what You have

I want to live where You live

Your people will be my people

    And Your spiritual Way of Life

        My spiritual Way of life and living.

CHAPTER FOUR

God's Invitation—A Life in Harmony with the Spirit that is Holy

We have examined the key role of Natural Law in our life and living and how the new discoveries of Biophysics and the Zero Point Field play their role in God's revelation of spiritual truth. These are part of our sensory world, however invisible some of the parts may be to our human eyes. But as was stated in our premise, we humans are more than atoms, molecules and energy fields. We have a spiritual essence, which we sometimes call our soul. And it is that spiritual essence, which is the essential me, that will one day leave my physical body and journey into the Spiritual World.

The world may deny or attempt to explain away our spiritual essence but we who walk the Way of life with Jesus know it very well. Furthermore, we are aware at times of Angels, spirits and the metaphysical world. Our Heavenly Creator, Himself invisible, has provided the help we need in order for our spiritual essence to develop into something that can inherit eternity after our cycle of physical living has ended. That is His Plan. (See Appendix One)

Through His Will He has given us many avenues whereby we can learn how and what we need to be and do so that our soul may develop into something of its potential in preparation for eternity. As Jesus said, "It is the spirit that gives life, the flesh profits nothing." (John 6:63) Our spiritual life is designed to grow and develop even as our physical bodies obey the law of entropy and eventually die.

The special coming of the Spirit that is Holy

Our spiritual development is unique and special, suited to the unique and one-of-a-kind person that is each human. To meet this personal need God sent the Holy Spirit into our world, into our unconscious, with its connection to the Zero Point Field, as discussed in the last chapter.

The Holy Spirit has been a part of the creation from the beginning. It is mentioned in the first verses of the Bible. But after Jesus, the Messenger from God, came into our world, lived and taught the Message of truth, was arrested, crucified but then resurrected and ascended into Heaven, the third member of the Holy Trinity, the Spirit that is Holy, made a special entrance into our world. It now dwells in the unconscious of every human, rising into our consciousness for guidance and empowerment for spiritual living—commonly referred to as our "conscience."

The Holy Paraclete

Jesus told His disciples, before He left this earth, that they were to wait in Jerusalem until the Holy Spirit came to them. (John 14:16-20) Jesus said it would be a Holy "Paraclete." (John 14:16, footnote, original Greek) A paraclete was the name given to a slave who was assigned to take care of a child, to see that they did what they were supposed to do, and to protect them. We call this Spirit of Holiness the Holy Ghost, Holy Spirit, but how about using the name Jesus used, which explains what this member of the Holy Trinity is and does—the Holy Paraclete? This name describes what His role is in our lives. Jesus said this Holy Paraclete would teach us what we need to know and bring to our remembrance what He said and did. (John 14:26)

This Holy Paraclete arrived on the Jewish thanksgiving holiday which we call Pentecost. Its physical manifestations were a mighty wind and tongues of fire which rested on each one of the disciples. They began to speak in various languages.

These physical manifestations are so important to us sensory bound humans. The mighty wind was associated with the breath of God, which resides in our body as our soul. Fire was, and is, a cleansing agent. We are cleansed from our sins by the death of Jesus. Now we can learn to witness God's truth with a cleansed tongue!

Finally, the disciples spoke languages, not glossolalia. The disciples remembered how humans once tried to build the Tower of Babel to Heaven (Genesis 11:1-9) but were frustrated by not having a common language so they could communicate with each other. Now the universal language of love in the Jesus Message was to bind the human ethnic groups together, not to build a tower <u>to</u> Heaven but to disperse the Jesus Message <u>from</u> Heaven throughout the earth.

The dwelling place of the Holy Paraclete

As stated above, this Holy Paraclete dwells in the unconscious of every human. We sometimes call it our conscience. It rises into our consciousness with moral directives and the empowerment to follow those directives. If we commit to following our Lord Jesus we will listen to this Paraclete as it attempts to guide and empower us in the Jesus way of Life through love.

It is a gentle, silent voice. It is never clamorous or demanding. It can best be described as an awareness. It is easy to ignore this "voice." The more we ignore it, the greater the difficulty we will have in hearing it.

Everyone has difficulty taking the necessary time out, learning to be silent and humble so they can "hear" this voice; be aware of this "voice." Being humble and teachable (Beatitude 1, Matthew 5:3), taking the time to pray and meditate, being by oneself, often in the night, facilitates our awareness. The right attitude was expressed to the boy Samuel when he was told to respond to the Lord's awareness with the words, "Speak, Lord, for your servant is listening." (I Samuel

3:10) It goes without saying that the words of the Spirit that is Holy are always gentle, loving, harmonious messages, in total harmony with Natural Law and the love commandment of Jesus.

The "other" voices

Any honest observation of our living will lead us to realize that there is not only the gentle goodness of the Spirit that is Holy in our world, but there is that which is strident, destructive, insistent; tempting us with false promises which invariably lead to chaos. There is the Holy Spirit but there are also unholy spirits which are out of harmony with the fundamental order of this creation in which we live and is therefore at cross purposes with the Sustaining Will. To follow them is always a disaster!

Why were such "spirits" allowed into our world? Strange as it may seem, as briefly discussed above, it is for our benefit! It is God's plan that any human who wishes can walk the Way of Life through love for their salvation. For this "walk" our Holy Paraclete provides the guidance and the empowerment, allowing us to become a spiritual being capable of living in eternity. But to be able to live in that wonderful environment, our Creator had to be sure we wouldn't some day rebel and ruin the New Heaven and the New Earth as the present earth has been ruined!

It is an adage that if the human race were asked how many want to go to Heaven, everyone would raise their hand. If they were told that they would have to learn how to walk the Narrow Path of God's righteousness, learn to lay aside self by learning how to sacrifice in love, learn to lay aside their own will and their own ideas of how-it-is in order to learn how it really is according to God's Will, many people would demur. Others may try out that Narrow Way but will later forsake it for their own ideas of how it is or ought to be by their standards. See the Parable of the Sower. This parable is so important that it is in all three synoptic Gospels, Matthew 13:1-9, 18-23, Mark 4:1-12, Luke 8:4-10.

Sin also serves

But sin also serves. Every human is given the right of choice. Those who seek the righteousness of God, which is based upon living in harmony with Natural Law based upon a spirit of love and love of the truth above all else, will, through their daily this-not-that choices, grow into a being which can live in the world of absolute love in which the Deity dwells. The Way of Life through love is a sanctification process of day by day following by faith the Good Shepherd now and into the eternity of the Spiritual World.

In a way sin makes no sense. Why would anyone listen to the sometimes seductive, sometimes strident, insistent, tempting voices which, when followed, always lead to chaos, when they can be a part of love, order and harmony? How many times do we have to be burned before we reject the ways that don't work in this world?

The big question

Our problem is not avoiding sin so we won't go to Hell; it is what do we really want out of life? Do we want the things of God? Do we want what Jesus has to offer? Do we want it enough to lay aside everything else to achieve it? If what Jesus has to offer is what we want, God has given us the revelations and power we need to achieve it.

We have the witness of the truth in the law and order of this creation, the witness of the life and teachings of Jesus and the witness of our own conscience through the indwelling Holy Spirit, the Holy Trinity. We have the witness of the ministering Holy Angels. We also have the witness of the experiences of the followers throughout human history. All we have to do is commit to following the Way day by day. Our Holy Paraclete is present to guide and empower us for this adventure of faith.

The key to it all is the individual will of every human. Our Creator couldn't give us the right to choose correctly without giving us the ability to choose badly. All real choices have at least two alternatives. But why would He give us this choice? To provide a Way through which we humans can develop into something very special!

It is so important to realize that our Creator could not give us the ability to choose righteousness without giving us the ability to choose behavior patterns contrary to Natural Law as expressed in the Ten Commandments with its foundation on the Way of Life through love as lived and taught by Jesus. The absolute consequences of sin are spiritual and sometimes physical death. How could it be otherwise? So why would our Creator create humans with this deadly potential?

We are more than pets

God has all the plants and animals He could ever want to love and care for in this creation. Each are fulfilling their programmed niche. Love that is programmed, as in a dog or cat, is wonderful but limited. God apparently wanted love from a creature that has choice. A love that says "Yes," when it can say "No," is much stronger than a love that is programmed to say "Yes." Furthermore, a love that desires to say "Yes," when there are all kinds of temptations to avoid the yes commitment, becomes a much stronger commitment. That's us.

We live in a cycle of life into which are many continual choices of this-not-that. Every choice adds up to something. At any time we are the sum of our choices. This is the iron law of the reign of Jesus mentioned so many times in the book of Revelation. (Revelation 2:27, 12:5, 19:15) As we chose so shall we become. (Galatians 6:7) What could make more common sense—we become what we choose in the daily process of living out our lives. We have been given the Ten Commandments, the life and teachings of Jesus, the indwelling presence of our Holy Paraclete and the ministry of the Holy Angels. We have the history of our ancestors as a guide. Everyone chooses, some to live a spiritual life based on love while living in their cycle of life on earth but others won't!

The personal presence of the Spirit that is Holy

A special Presence, the Spirit that is Holy, is our umbilical cord to spiritual life. It is our <u>personal</u> guide and empowerment as it attempts to get us to follow the goodness of the Holy Will.

The work of our Holy Paraclete is simple: To get us to follow the Ten Commandments as simplified versions of Natural Law and to get us to open to the energy forces of the light of love, the Will of the Source, as expressed through the Zero Point Field about and within us and to accept by faith the gift of salvation in Jesus. We do this because we want it. It works for the order and harmony in the life of anyone who so chooses. Why would anyone choose the consequences of disobedience to the consequences of goodness? This is not a neutral universe!

Our ongoing spiritual struggle

Everyone is engaged in an ongoing personal spiritual struggle between following the Spirit that is Holy and following the unholy spirits. No exceptions! The Bible calls it the Battle of Armageddon. (Revelation 16:16) Call the evil spirits what we will, Lucifer, Satan, evil, jinns, devils, whatever, the adversarial temptations and diversions from God's standard of reality and goodness based on love existentially exist. They are a reality and the consequences of their activity in humans is sin, rebellion and chaos. Again, it's reality! These experienced temptations tend to center around three personal arenas.

Basic temptations: #1 - feeding the body only or also our soul

Many churches begin the Lenten Season before Easter with meditations on the three temptations of Jesus which become our temptations. (Matthew 4:1-11) The first is: Do we feed the body only or will we feed our spiritual essence, our soul as well? Our body needs food, shelter and clothing. It has its aches and illnesses, its chemically driven desires and its self-centered view of the world. We can spend our life-span on earth caring and feeding physical needs to the exclusion of that part of our life, our spiritual essence, which is the only thing that will be me when I lay aside my physical body. Jesus said that we don't live by bread alone but by every word that proceeds from the mouth of God. (Matthew 4:4) Simple common sense! What foolishness to spend all our time and resources on that which is perishing, and will some day perish, to the loss of what was designed to develop into an eternal spiritual being!

God's will or our will

Temptation #2 - The struggle between our will and the Will of God. Will we walk God's Way of Life through love via the crucifixion of our wrong attitudes, passions and willfulness or live by our own plan of how-it-is? In Jesus' case, would He come floating down into the Temple square upheld by angels and so prove that He was the Messenger from Heaven, or would He go the way of crucifixion, dying for the sins of the human race? Will we find life through God's way or try to find it by some substitute, some nothingness provided by the Destroyer of our souls? It is our daily struggle: God's way or my way!

God's Kingdom or Satan's

Temptation #3—Will we elect to be a part of God's Kingdom or slide along through life following our natural desires and the ways of the world? Unless we choose to follow God's Way, the Spirit directed way, daily, hourly, we naturally remain part of the world's way, sliding down the Broad Highway. We are to dwell in Heaven while sojourning on earth during our pilgrimage in our physical body. We choose, not once and for all, but continually, by our daily living, our everyday choices, whether we are a citizen of the Kingdom of light and love, living a life of separation, or being part of those who will not make the separation, will not lead a Spirit directed life.

There is a terrible delusion that having a one time experience, commitment, such as being baptized or being "saved," some religious experience, we have our ticket punched for Heaven. Our spiritual life is a matter of continual day-by-day growth, not a one-time event as if we are joining a country club! Unless we will continually choose the light we will slide back slowly into the darkness. Change is inevitable, but which way?

The Lord's Prayer

These temptations were with Jesus every day of His sojourn on earth. Those same temptations are with us every day of our cycle of living. Key to the success of our ability to live in harmony with Natural Law and the love basis of Jesus is our prayer life. How often do we talk with God, not just "to God," but with God? Lovers communicate.

Too often we wait for some crisis before we pray a hasty prayer for help. This love-bond God wants to have with us is the basis of our prayer-life. So what do we say?

The Lord's Prayer is a perfect model. (Matthew 6:9-13) Listen to what Jesus taught us to say. We begin by addressing our "Heavenly Father." The Deity is not some lordly dictator, some willful potentate, He is our Father, not just our Creator. He has a father's love; a father's sustaining love.

"Holy is Your Name," Yahveh Jireh—the God who Provides. We believe in His Name, the God Who Provides, therefore we are asking by faith for what follows.

We then acknowledge God's sustaining Will. "Your Kingdom come, Your Will be done on earth as it is in Heaven." We want to be in harmony with that Will. We pledge ourselves to do all we can to facilitate that Will, including our immediate concerns.

"Give us this day our daily bread." We ask for food for our soul as well as food for our body in this existential moment, this now, of our living.

"Forgive us our trespasses." We acknowledge that we are unworthy to ask anything of the Lord of this Creation because of our sins of commission and especially omission.

"As we forgive those who trespass against us!" That's the clincher— forgive us as we forgive those who have trespassed against us. No forgiveness = no forgiveness!

"Deliver us from evil." Only the strength and power of God can deliver us from the temptations which beset us. He provides the means, we provide the commitment.

When His disciples asked Jesus to teach them how to pray, He gave them this prayer. It is a model. We add to, or elaborate upon it, based on the Jesus promise that if we ask we will receive, if we seek we will find, if we knock the way will be opened for us. (Matthew 7:7) God has four answers to our prayers: "Yes!" "No, I cannot in love give it to you!" "No, not now, but later when you are able to receive it!" "No, I have something better for you!" Every prayer is answered by one of these responses.

Praying is so much more than "gimme" prayers. Prayers, such as the Lord's Prayer, places us in a special relationship with the One Who Provides. It is a sharing of a love-bond, a trust, which grows with usage. It is our faith in action.

How often should we pray? At least at the beginning and ending of each day, but also any time in between when we need to get our head on straight. Prayer is part of our spiritual umbilical cord into the presence of the Sustainer from which we draw the light energy of love. We cannot draw too often upon this spiritual sustenance; this love energy from the Source.

We choose this-not-that every moment of our existence. We may complain, with some justification, of our inability to know all the choice factors clearly, for we seldom do. But we have our attitudes, our mind sets, and they form the basis of our choices. To realize why we did or thought so and so, we must examine our attitudes, our mind sets.

Our spiritual examination

At some level we know something of good and evil and love. Everyone needs love in order to function well during their cycle of existence upon this earth. No one has it perfectly. In our hearts we know that to have love we must give it; that we get as we give what we have, the quid pro quo of life.

But we carry with us an enormous baggage of attitudes, biases and points-of-view. Everyone has them. Everyone has a unique set. It is our personal set that determines how much and the degree of accuracy of what we perceive as the teachings of our Holy Paraclete that we will actually hear. Furthermore, that baggage determines so much of what we will do with what we hear.

The Baggage of our developing years

It begins in our childhood. Various psychologists have names for the stages of human development. I shall use the Sensori-motor, from birth to the development of language, the Age of Magic from learning language to the development of the left hemisphere of the brain during the ages four to six, the development of the left hemisphere in the Concrete Operational, which extends into the sub-teens, Teen-age Socialization, which climaxes during our teens and, finally, the establishment of a Belief System during the teens and young adulthood. We will carry our experiences and perspectives gained during these five stages of development into the adult choice-making process every day of our living. This early learning is the basis of what and how we will respond to the voice of the Holy Paraclete within us throughout our adult years.

During our Sensori-motor time we are dependent upon the big people for everything. A child interprets having their needs met as love. Did we learn to trust the provisions of our care givers at the beginning of our living or didn't we? Fears of abandonment will haunt us. We will have a hard time trusting God if we didn't learn to early on trust the big people of our lives for our needs.

Age of Magic children learn how to relate to the big people—obey and get the cookies, disobey and you get some form of punishment. They will deal with this concept of morality throughout their adult living. Their worth is determined by their obedience!

Age of Magic children are dominated by the right hemisphere of their brain. Magic is all about them. Gooey messes are turned into cookies! The border line between the physical and the metaphysical is very fluid. Prayer is easy. Make believe personages are very real. Love, expressed through the care of the big people, is essential for children of this age. Jesus said we are to have this spiritual sensitivity if we are to ever perceive the Kingdom of God. (Matthew 18:3) Without that love development, fear, anxiety, hatred and feelings of worthlessness can become dominant emotions.

Concrete Operational aged children become left brain dominated. They learn sensory reality. Reality is measured by the five senses! Santa Clauses and tooth-fairies fade away! The realization develops that a nickel will not buy a candy bar no matter how much it is wanted. Too often ridicule about spiritual matters allows the child to jettison the whole matter of the unseen Age of Magic world. Later, in adult life, faith becomes very difficult for individuals who have completely rejected the imaginative world.

It is part of the Creator's plan that in old age the left hemisphere begins to fade but we retain and even strengthen the spiritual imagery of the right hemisphere. We begin life and we end our cycle of life where we need to be, able to think in terms of spiritual realities. It is also why, as quoted above, Jesus could say that unless we became as little children we will never perceive the Kingdom of God.

A child's social development proceeds along the lines of playing by themselves with others, to pals, to a group, to a significant other. If the need for love from adult care givers is not met they may retreat into a recluse unwilling to venture again into any kind of love-bond with another. Being spurned by love-bonding attempts can lead to a refusal to make the effort of adventuring into the love arena again. How difficult it is for such wounded individuals to open to the love light of life; to live a fulfilled life in this core foundation needed for living well! How easy to adopt behavior patterns that seem to not need love-bonding with the opposite sex!

During the last years of childhood the child forms a belief system upon which they will make their decisions for the rest of their adult years. That it is biased is a given. That it is inadequate is also a given. The adult years are designed to change and augment that belief system so that it is in greater harmony with reality. That humility and teachableness is key to that growth as stated in the first of the Beatitudes: "Blessed are the humble for theirs is the Kingdom of God." (Matthew 5:3)

As a reaction to troubling adult experiences many will retreat to one of the earlier childhood phases and stay there. It has been discovered through tests, that three-fourths of the adults think and behave as if they were ten to twelve years of age. Some may retreat so far as to become once more a curled up fetus in a mental institution!

Living with our set of personal characteristics

Everyone lives out their cycle of life with their own unique set of genes, environments and their learning experiences. That they will change through the choices made during the many daily cycles of living is a given. To guide and empower correct choices is the work of our Holy Paraclete in our lives. The Will of the Creator sustains the order of this world. We determine, by our choices, how that Will enables our personal lives. Will it be heard? Will we obey? What is the status of our prayer life? Will we provide the conditions needed so our spiritual essence and our physical body will be able to hear and obey the Spirit that is Holy within us?

Opening to the Holy Spirit

We need to recognize a "true fact" here. We think of ourselves as searching for love and truth. In a way this is true but the reality is the reverse. The Holy Will is the omnipresent God, all about us and within us. Will we open to it? Will we allow what it tells us to do to happen? Will we get rid of the obstacles, the actions and the attitudes which make it so difficult for us to hear and obey the silent voice of our Holy Paraclete?

Through out all of our living, it is God who seeks us, it is His Holy Will that surrounds us. The indwelling Holy Spirit is ever seeking to be heard and followed. "Let go and let God" becomes a byword for our spiritual growth and development for those experienced in the faith. Our spiritual development led by our Holy Paraclete will happen if we allow it. We need never pray for God to be with us for He is omnipotent, omniscient and omnipresent. The question is ever and continually, "Are we with God?"

Do we really want the spiritual dimension in our lives?

Fundamentally, we need love. We want—but whatever we want is colored by our developmental years which preceded the present moment. We want something more than we have. But is that all? The spiritually sensitive can discern something vastly more—a desire, a guidance, an inner voice, a yearning for something positive, beautiful and fulfilling. We experience that voice as a silent call to holiness, wholeness. Through the silent voice within, we are experiencing the voice of the Spirit that is Holy.

We are in a struggle between that which is in harmony with Natural Law as sustained by the light, love energy of the Will of the One, and behavior that isn't. Evil tempts us into behavior patterns that don't work on the long run in this creation as it is made. We call it evil! We despair! We have feelings we don't like, such as hatred. We can perceive potentials of worth and goodness toward which we cannot find an avenue. We are depressed. But is that all? Can we recognize the desire of our Holy Father to help us through such experiences? We are not alone unless we choose to be!

Resurrection Power

Part of the power of the Zero Point Field is exerted in the ability of nature to right itself. Wounds heal. A broken tree reasserts itself in its growth toward light and life. Resurrections and renewals are built into the cycles of our living. Every cycle, day, week and season of our living, our trials, our valleys, come to an end so a new cycle can begin. As we begin a new cycle we are designed to lay aside the old, turn a new leaf and greet new possibilities at each new beginning with a positive attitude of faith. We cannot relive our yesterdays and live well in our existential moments today!

Jesus provides resurrections, new beginnings for our human needs, but most importantly, new beginnings are available for each individual who will accept this gift by their faith. Are we willing to believe in the One Who Provides, however deep and dark the valley; believe that Jesus is with us? Do we accept the possibility of an end to the dark valleys of experience and the possibility of a new beginning? Will we allow the light of life through love as offered to us through the Will of our Heavenly Sustainer to energize us for a new dawn? It is all there for us, thanks to the guidance and empowerment of the Holy Spirit and God's ministering hands through the Holy Angels. The key is our faith. Without our faith it can't happen!

When we "let go and let God," things begin to happen. The empowerment for change is offered by our indwelling Spirit that is Holy but are we willing to seek it? Do we believe it? Do we really want to believe it? We need to cross that faith bridge into the spiritual realities of God, our loving Provider. No crossing, no resurrection!

Noise

Too many people, perhaps everyone at times, can not become aware of this inner "voice" because of the constant "noise" in which they immerse themselves in their living. It takes stillness and quietude, the peace of the Presence, for us to be able to hear this voice from the Spiritual World. For too many people, this experience of guidance from spiritual sources seldom, if ever, occurs. It is simply drowned out in the cacophony of their living. That does not mean it is not there, it simply means that they can't hear it!

It cannot be too strongly stressed that "noise" tends to obscure the spiritual voice. It is a hard reality that when we deliberately obliterate outside noise we can also drown out the inner voice of the Holy Spirit. One can elect to go through life on a sea of noise, music, voices and entertainment broadcasts and seldom be conscious of the inner life.

For the spiritually attuned this resurrection power is precious, real and a positive directive in the storms of life. Faith in God's resurrection power provides the stability needed to be in harmony with Natural Law and especially for spiritual bonding with the Intelligence, the light, love, energy connection to the Will. As we "let go and let God," we allow renewed faith to build within us. Positive attitudes, a new mind set, begins to emerge if we will allow it by our faith in the One Who Provides. Much time in prayer; more time in focusing on the positive, will build new perspectives. God offers us this resurrection power through the Holy Spirit. It is there for us if we choose to use it.

What more can one ask than to live in blessed harmony with the realities of God's larger life? It is there for the accepting but it won't happen until we take the journey of faith and accept the Way of Life through Love as offered by the Deity Who Provides, Yahweh Jireh. Distracting noise, piped in music, focusing on anxieties and hatreds, guarantees limited connections with the silent voice of God.

The Messenger Savior from God

But to understand spiritual realities we humans needed someone to come from the Spiritual World, enter into our life and living and give us the truth. That person was and is the historical Jesus. Jesus existed, and for those who choose to follow His Way of Life through love, He is very present in our world and in our personal lives today.

Again, this is not a matter of "if you believe its true for you but its not true for me, therefore it doesn't exist!" Jesus is an historical figure. What was recorded about Him is not just someone's wishes, it happened! How do we know? It is still happening today precisely as Jesus said it would. At any moment one can elect to walk by faith the Jesus Way of Life through love, allow the energy flow of light and love to flow into us and begin to experience precisely what was experienced two thousand years ago.

The Spiritual World is not like an on/off button for our television set. The Holy Spirit is to be our constant connection with spiritual reality. However, we can elect to shut it all off, disengage from spiritual reality, live in some virtual world spun by some paid program organizer, float through our one-time cycle of existence and lose all that our Creator designed for us to enjoy. It is our choice.

History is real. Our history has consequences! We are part of what has and is actually happening. Life is not a "Star-trek" fantasy! What is happening now will be history in a moment! And once recorded no amount of wishful thinking can undo it!

It is again the reality of what Jesus did and said that concerns us. Humans can say this or that, believe this or that, but it is the reality of the life and the teachings of Jesus that concern us. Truth from the Spirit that is Holy is reality, it is actually happening! It is not some historical fiction!

As promised, the Holy Paraclete will teach us the Message Jesus brought from Heaven to Earth. Jesus, the Messenger of God with the truth, gave us Five Imperatives. Let us examine them.

Imperative One: Loving as Jesus loved us

We are to love one another by the standard of how Jesus loved us. (John 13:34, 15:12, 17) We are His followers only by so doing! We have a record of what He did, His healing, His caring, His response to needs, His respect for the individual and His understanding of life situations; our definition of love. Love is the basis of His Message as it is the basis of the light and life of this creation in which we live. What else is more important, given the conditions and the needs under which we humans live?

Imperative Two: Living in perfect harmony with God's Law

We are to live in perfect harmony with Natural Law as expressed through the Will of the One. (Matthew 5:48) What else could any true spiritual messenger say? The Law exists, breakages, however slight, always contribute to chaos. Natural Law, including the Zero Point Field, not only exists but controls every aspect of this creation. How could it be otherwise and this world function in the fantastic order of its existence?

Imperative Three: Seeking first God's Kingdom and His righteousness

Since we have a spiritual essence which will one day leave our bodies and journey into the Spiritual World, that essence should have the priority of our attention and care while we live in our physical body. The spiritual must have dominance over the physical if we are to find the life which is life indeed. (Matthew 6:33) As stated above, the first temptation facing everyone is to prioritize the body over the spiritual. It is our physical body that declines in life-energy. It is our spiritual essence that is designed to grow in that energy.

Imperative Four: Being as merciful as God is merciful

Since we are fallible human beings, since we need a positive attitude in dealing with our shortcomings, we need an attitude of mercy toward ourselves and toward other fallible humans. (Luke 6:36) Without mercy humans cannot live in harmony with other humans or themselves. Merciless attitudes lead to attitudes of worthlessness, quarrelsomeness and bigotry. Jesus addressed this issue in the Fifth Beatitude: "Blessed are the merciful, for they shall obtain mercy." (Matthew 5:7)

Imperative Five: Loving and praying for our enemies

We are to love our enemies and pray for those who wrongfully use us. (Matthew 5:44, Luke 6:27, 28) How else can we build a stable and positive society? Under the injunction of eye for an eye and a tooth for a tooth everyone would eventually be blind and toothless!

Is this a new set of laws replacing the Ten Commandments? No way. What function do they play in our lives? They are key to living under the Gospel Covenant.

The Motivation for living under the Gospel Covenant

Here we must examine a basic difference in our motivation for living the Jesus Way under the Gospel Covenant and the motivation for living under the old Law Covenant. These imperatives are not a new set of laws augmenting the Ten Commandments. So what are they? They are part of the precious Gospel Covenant.

Under the Law Covenant, under which every human begins life, is the ethical system which every child understands: Obey the big people and get the cookies, disobey and you're in trouble!

This is what God told Adam and Eve. It is the basis of our existence under Natural Law. It is simply expressed in the Ten Commandments. It is expressed in the Bible as in this passage from Deuteronomy, "See,

I have set before you today life and prosperity, death and adversity; in that I command you today to love the Lord your God, to walk in His ways and to keep His commandments and His statutes and His judgments, that you may live and multiply, and that the Lord your God may bless you in the land where you are entering to possess it. But if your heart turns away and you will not obey, but are drawn away and worship other gods and serve them, I declare to you today that you shall surely perish." (Deuteronomy 30:15-18)

But, as stated earlier, we obviously cannot perfectly obey. We need another covenant if we are ever to find the Way of Life. And God provided that other covenant, the Gospel covenant. It was made possible by Jesus' death on Calvary. It was foretold in that gristly story of Abraham's sacrifice of his son Isaac. (Genesis 22:1-14)

Before we understand the great truth contained in this story, let us look at another fundamental principle—how are we to read the Bible? Jesus said over and over again that we need to be careful <u>how</u> we read the Bible, not, do we read it, but how do we read it? (Luke 818, 10:26)

So how are we to read this repulsive story? The story of Abraham's sacrifice of his son Isaac is a teaching story, a profound teaching story, but it is just that, a teaching story, a myth. If we think of it as literal history, then we will miss the point of the story. Let's look at the details. God told Abraham to sacrifice his son. God gave us the Sixth Commandment, "You shall do no murder!" How can God be quoted as commanding one thing and then demanding another? Therefore this is not history but a teaching story! Abraham and Isaac journeyed three days to the mount prescribed for the sacrifice, which is the mountain upon which the Temple would later be built in Jerusalem. Isaac carried the wood for the sacrifice. At the last moment a ram is offered instead of Isaac.

This story is another prophesy of Jesus—the three days journey and his carrying the cross of wood are part of the Jesus story. Finally Jesus becomes the ram offered in place of Isaac, in place of we sinners. But why all this? It is key to understanding God!

This story exists because of the name Abraham gave God—Yahweh Jireh in Hebrew—God will provide! That becomes the name of God in the Bible. The Deity is the One who provides everything we have, everything that happens and everything that is, beginning with the sacrifice of Jesus for our sins—the Gospel Covenant. He is the Creator and the Sustainer of life through that Gospel Covenant.

Because of the sacrifice of Jesus for our sins we stand in Jesus, our Savior, before God, as though we had never sinned. We have a new relationship with God. We no longer obey God out of fear of trespasses which would send us to Hell, a relationship that could not provide our salvation; we obey God out of love and thanksgiving for what He has <u>provided.</u>

It is the way of life Jesus laid before Peter: Do you love <u>Me</u> more than these things? Are you committed to <u>Me </u>in love? Are you <u>My</u> friend? (phileus me, in Greek) (John 21:15-17)

Life in Jesus

The essence of the teaching of the Holy Spirit is very simple—our life is to be found in and through Jesus. We follow this Good Shepherd through love of what He lived and taught. Jesus is not only a teacher, someone who lived in such a way that we can ask ourselves in a moral dilemma, "What would Jesus do?," but key to it all, He is the sacrificial Lamb of God taking the consequences of our sins upon Himself. The world makes fun of this but what does that matter? It happened. Jesus, the Son of God, was crucified. We <u>experience</u> the resurrected life made possible by Jesus. We <u>experience</u> the flow of the life-giving love, energy, light from the Will of the Source when the obstacles of disbelief, skepticism and narrow tunnel-vision concepts of life are removed along with the consequences of our moral missteps.

This life in Jesus is not just pleasant theology, wishful thinking or just a diversion from ugly reality; it is a magnificent way of living that actually works. Every time one has committed themselves to the Jesus Way of Life through love, sought to live out their spiritual citizenship by commitment, accepted the Jesus gift of life by faith and learned to yield to the light energy field of love of the Will, great changes occur, new life beckons, new vistas of living open up. It works!

Amazingly enough, it is in the temptations of evil, the work of evil in our lives and it the world around us, that brings home to most people the jarring reality of the spiritual world. People may not engage the goodness of the spiritual world but the reality of the evil world of death, destruction and the temptations to be part of it, are real to every human! Unless we actively engage the truths of Jesus we will slide on through life focused on nothingnesses which will erode, little by little and day by day, our capacity to engage and grow in the truth, love and beauty of the Jesus Message. Sin also serves!

Jesus was divine. His resurrection power was exhibited during His ministry, as well as in every life of any human who has committed themselves to His Way of Life through love ever since. That power demonstrates that He is more than human, He is real—today, at this moment! Not just by affirming it to be so, but experientially, in our existential living. As His followers, we experience the love of the risen Jesus day by day. Being more than human He could be the substitutionary atonement for the sins of all. Being human He could be a human sacrifice for His fellow humans. Jesus is the Messenger of God with the Message (the Logos) from God. He is the central figure in all human history, giving meaning to it all. That some don't choose to believe it is totally irrelevant to the reality of Jesus' role, both in history and at this moment!

Jesus gives meaning to human history

In the second vision of the book of Revelation, a quandary is presented in Heaven. (Revelation 5:1f) There is a book of human history in the hand of the Creator but no one can open or make sense of it. Only Jesus can open the book, break its seven seals.

A great truth is presented here—Jesus the Christ, the Messiah, gives meaning to human existence, the purpose of human creation.

His life and teachings are based upon Natural Law, providing the means, through His sacrifice, whereby we humans can fulfill it. He did not come to replace the Commandments but to fulfill them in our stead. (Matthew 5:17, 18) Once fulfilled, they become our guide in the new life guaranteed by the Gospel Covenant. His five Imperatives, recorded above, provide goals for our spiritual development under the Gospel Covenant. In Jesus, we humans can learn how to assume our role in the larger symphony of this creation.

His love commandment is to provide the basis for our living. We commit to that kind of love as the number one priority for our living. We learn how to love by the Jesus standard, not some human standard. The ideal is to develop a love-bond with Jesus, become a friend of the Creator and Sustainer and living, through Jesus, in compliance with the sustaining Will. Jesus is designed to be our Good Shepherd. The life, the ethic, the sacrifice, the quality of the life of Jesus gives the final meaning to human history, to our personal history. All human potential, personal and social, is to be measured by that standard if we are going to understand the reason for our existence.

Understanding human history

The first of those seven "seals" to understanding human history, as revealed in the book of Revelation (Chapter 6), is this simple fact: the life and teachings of Jesus (Seal #1) are the measurement standard for solving all human problems: wars (Seal #2), famines (Seal, #3) giving meaning to premature deaths (Seal #4), the why of martyrdom (Seal #5), the meaning of natural disasters (Seal #6) and the various judgments of God (Seal #7, Rev. Chapters 7-18).

Without the Jesus standard what meaning does human existence have? By what standard do we understand the meaning of wars, famines, premature deaths, martyrdom of goodness, natural disasters and the realities of the Creator's choices in this world in which we find ourselves? Why listen to human understandings when we have the Messenger from God with the Message of life? His Way makes such common sense!

The major premise for understanding of our reason for being

The Messenger from Heaven provides the standard of evaluation as to the meaning of the events which comprise human history, personal and social. Jesus provides the measurement for understanding the why of our existence and what we can do to rectify the behavior that caused the events of history. Living by the Jesus standard guarantees the quality of life our Creator meant for every human when He created Homo sapiens. A social model based upon people seeking the Jesus Way of Life through love guarantees the best of all possibilities. That most won't do it is key to our problems!

Wishful thinking?

But again, is this nothing more than wishful thinking? It is the experience of reality to all who will be part of that energy flow from the Source made possible by Jesus. People can choose to be skeptics, can choose attitudes of disbelief, but why dwell in those mind sets when the positive, the beautiful, the good and the workable can be part of anyone's resurrected living? Simply following the teachings of Jesus would solve all human problems. It is as simple as that! We make our choices and those choices all have consequences. Isn't it but common sense to choose that which works, that which makes life more beautiful, that which enriches our lives and those around us?

This was once but a matter of faith and faith's experiences, but now, through our knowledge of the Zero Point field, we have empirical evidence of the physical reality of all of this. It is God's blessed loving Will that created and sustains this world. It is Jesus, the Messenger from God with the Message from God, who is the key figure around which all human understandings of how-it-is must be built if we wish to have a real basis for living well in this creation in which we find ourselves! Jesus is the physical expression of Divine Will.

The eternal therefore

The result? We follow Jesus and the One Who Provides. In thankfulness we strive to more fully fulfill the Jesus imperatives. We will never be perfect. That is not the point. Jesus has fulfilled the Law in our stead. (Matthew 5:17, 18) We have the attitudes that make the Gospel Covenant journey possible. It is being on the journey that counts!

As stated above, so much rests upon our attitudes! There are eight candidates for the attitudes we need if we are going to live well in this world in which we find ourselves! (Matthew 5:1-12) Attitudes make all the difference. These eight attitudes, the Beatitudes, begin the only complete sermon we have of Jesus; which begins the New Testament. Important!

The Eight Blessed attitudes(Beatitudes)

Attitude One. "Blessed are the humble (the teachable), for theirs is the Kingdom of Heaven."

In order to live as a citizen of God's Kingdom we need to be teachable, willing to learn what is needed, humble in our attitude of what we think we know. How else can we make use of the ongoing cycles of our living in a positive manner? To assume that our finite minds have it all figured out and need no change, shortcuts the purpose of the cyclical processes of our natural world and blunts the energy flow of the Will into those who have erected the various blockages—none more absolute than the attitude that we already know what we need to know!

Attitude Two. "Blessed are those who mourn, for they shall be comforted."

In order to live as a citizen of God's Kingdom we need to recognize that there is so much more available for us and mourn over the simple fact that we too often choose and are satisfied with so much less than we could or should be. Spiritual laziness leads to spiritual inertness!

Attitude Three. "Blessed are the gentle, for they shall inherit the earth."

In order to live as a citizen of God's Kingdom we need a gentle, observant, inquisitive attitude, able to learn from the multitude of incidents going on around and within us. So shall we be able to live harmoniously in this environment in which we find ourselves. The gentle life style facilitates our spiritual development by utilizing the love, light, energy force field which makes possible our spiritual growth. With a gentle attitude we can learn to live in harmony with this natural world and inherit the new one to come!

Attitude Four. "Blessed are those who hunger and thirst for righteousness, for they shall be satisfied."

In order to live as a citizen of God's Kingdom we need to hunger for God's righteous standard of living that works in this world. We need an attitude of desiring the harmonious state of that standard and allowing that desire to commit us into doing the work necessary to achieve that state of spiritual feasting by removing the obstacles which inhibit the spiritual light, love and energy flow. We need to be hungry for what Jesus has to offer!

Attitude Five. "Blessed are the merciful, for they shall receive mercy."

In order to live as a citizen of God's Kingdom we need to have an attitude of mercy, as described above. A merciless attitude guarantees feelings of worthlessness within ourselves and a desire for removing any person or thing we believe stands in our way to a better life. The reality is that we are each one-of-a-kind. We need to recognize and be merciful to the rough edges within us and in the lives of those around us.

Attitude Six. "Blessed are the pure in heart, for they shall see God."

In order to live as a citizen of God's Kingdom we need to live a life committed to being in harmony with this creation of God as expressed in Natural Law and the Will of light and love energy which sustains life. Half-heartedness and half-measures guarantee that we will never see the purity of God's order and beyond that the One who makes it all possible. Jesus told the Laodicean type congregations that since they were luke-warm He would vomit them out of His mouth! (Revelation 3:16)

Attitude Seven. "Blessed are the peace-makers, for they shall be called the children of God."

In order to live as a citizen of God's Kingdom we must live peaceably. Strife, contention, fussing and wars, never, in themselves, lead to harmony. An attitude which desires peace leads to peace within ourselves regardless of the turmoil about us. The spiritual aura of peace emanating from us has a calming effect on those able to receive it. Those who pursue the avenues of peace are indeed blessed peacemakers for they make possible the hearing of the silent voice of the Holy Spirit within and about them. That peace must sometimes be achieved by removing the killers and the destroyers is a sad commentary on the quality of living some people choose for their behavior standards!

Attitude Eight. "Blessed are they who have been persecuted for the sake of righteousness, for theirs is the Kingdom of Heaven."

In order to live as a citizen of God's Kingdom we must accept the fact that if we choose to follow the Holy Spirit, those who don't make that choice will sometimes be upset with us. Rebellion wants company. If we choose to not be part of the actions which lead to chaos, we could be criticized, ostracized and even killed. If we are committed to making the choices which lead to peace, love and joy, to living in greater harmony with the sustaining Will, then we must forgive and love the spiritual essences, not the actions, of those who, but for the grace of God, we could be a part.

Our attitudes are key to our behavior patterns. Examine every sin and you will find an attitude behind the sin that made the sin possible. As mentioned above, there is an unseen spiritual force in this world, which we experience, which leads us into behavior that does not work on the long run for our personal or social welfare in this creation AS IT IS MADE BY ITS CREATOR. What may seem to work for a given moment will not work if everybody did it. (See the discussion on Kant's Categorical Imperative in Appendix Two) However justified, however explained or defined, the breakages of Natural Law and the resulting diminutive effect on our auras by negative behavior are well known to every human. Behavior deviating from Natural Law, as sustained by the Will from the Source, always shrinks our natural energy aura.

The Holy Angels

The God who Provides has given us not only the Holy Spirit but the ministrations of His Holy Angels to aid in our spiritual journey. Angels are mentioned two hundred and ninety-six times in the Bible. The Greek word, "angelos" which we have translated "angel," means "messenger." Angels are messengers from God. Jacob saw them in a dream going back and forth between Heaven and Earth on the business of God. (Genesis 28:12) They ministered to Jesus. (Matthew 4:11) Jesus will confess or deny us before the angels of God. (Luke 12:8, 9) Jesus promised Nathaniel that he would see the angels ascending and descending upon Jesus. (John 1:51) Angels are mentioned seventy-four times in the book of Revelation alone.

To treat the topic of angels under the idea that if we believe in them they exist but if we don't, they don't, is manifest foolishness.

We know the Zero Point Field exists although we will never see it. We know its reality by what it does. The same with these spiritual entities, the Holy Angels; we experience them. We also experience the temptations of evil spirits. They are very real, as are the Holy Angels. To the spiritually sensitive, angels become intensely real.

We sense them as power centers. As I am writing this I am aware of three such power centers about me. They are positive forces, guiding and enabling centers. I am also aware of a negative influence attempting to defuse the Will of my Sustaining Lord. I will continually make choices between them. I will continually choose, actively or passively, between the reality of goodness or the negative influences of evil, between reality and nothingness and between what works on the long run and what doesn't! It is the old temptation all over again: Will I elect to honor and obey my citizenship in God's spiritual kingdom or slide along with the herd down the Broad Highway?

To the inexperienced in spiritual matters it probably does not matter if the reality of spiritual entities are accepted or not, named or not, as long as it is realized that the struggle between the positive, the orderly, the beautiful and that which works for the negative, the lesser, is real. We have a choice as to how much of the Will of the Source we allow to become part of our living. There is always a choice. Life itself is choice making. That has been our definition of evil—that which does not work on the long run in this world which is based upon the order of Natural Law sustained by the Will of love, light and energy. It is our choice as to whether we will accept or reject the ways that not only give us life, but give it more abundantly. (John 10:10)

We experience the Holy Angels. Some experience them more than others. Their ministrations are real whether we accept or believe in them or not. How could any human belief system determine the existence of spiritual realities? Presumption indeed!

The Holy Angels seem to be part of the extended Will of the Intelligence in the development and furtherance of the order of this planet. What fun they must have had in developing the life entities which have existed and whatever is now part of our natural world!

The Bible says God spoke and it was done. (Genesis 1:3) How was it done? By the Holy Angels? They have been and are the specific ministers of the Sustaining and Creating Will which guided the development of life from the single cell to Homo sapiens. What could make more sense?

Many will scoff at this but then, what people have never experienced, or will not allow themselves to experience, cannot be part of their cognitive processes. If anyone chooses the good and the beautiful, that which functions in accord with Natural Law, they will experience these power centers, usually not visible to the naked eye but nonetheless they are very real. They desire to become our spiritual friends; present, loving and supportive friends, taking on molecular bodies only when needed for a specific situation. In order to develop our faith, it is desirable that we recognize these entities by our faith.

Why are some people never aware of them? Perhaps they are afraid of them! Perhaps they are uncomfortable having holy beings about them! Perhaps they are not looking with the right attitude. The Holy Angels are never intrusive or demanding presences. Whatever we believe has no effect on the existence of spiritual forces. Disbelief is a personal attitude which in no way influences reality except to the belief system of the attitude holder.

As one becomes more in harmony with the sustaining Will, as we allow the realities of the spiritual world to become a larger part of our life, these spiritual entities become more and more accepted realities of our living. As the love-bond builds, the unseen powers of the Spirit become ever more real, ever more an accepted part of the goodness of our Creator which we wish and want to be part of our lives. It is important to realize that spiritual awareness grows as we grow in the spirit. This journey of life is like ascending a mountain, the vistas grow as the ascent is made. We will never make it to the top while in our physical bodies, but it is the journey that counts.

The spiritual energy flow

The energy of the Zero Point Field is not just an inanimate flow, it is particularized through figures who are part of the Spiritual World, the Holy Angels, and the Spirit that is Holy. It is particularized in its encounters with each of us, caring for us, meeting our specific needs, providing resurrection power for renewed living and making us better channels of the energy flow of the Zero Point Field. Again, as we journey, as we allow ourselves to grow in our personal love-bond with Jesus, as we allow our spiritual essence to dominate our lives, changes occur, developments happen. Growth is key to life in this creation. It is like the mustard seed and yeast in the parables of Jesus. (Matthew 13:31-33) Our spiritual life is similar to a toboggan ride; we aren't certain as to where we are going moment by moment, but the ride is terrific!

The faith-based life

Once all this was a matter of faith, the experiential faith of the followers through the centuries. Now we have its reality offered to any who will open to the spirit-filled love energy Will of our Sustainer. But you don't try it out for thirty days and if it doesn't work you get your money back! Life is found first by loving the attitudes and ways of living taught by Natural Law and based on Jesus' love commandment. Love is opening up to the light energy of love through opening to the Will of the Source. We want what Jesus has to offer so much that we commit to that way of life. As we do so we learn the foundation of it all—the Jesus gift of salvation; which opens the way to learning how to love, how to be a person of love fed by the umbilical cord of the light energy of love through our connection with the Zero Point Field of the sustaining Will.

Our goal, as stated above, is to grow into a friendship type love-bond relationship with Jesus. (John 21:15-17) We experience it in bits and pieces, in moments on the mountain of beauty, truth and wholesomeness. We have the appetizers of the banquet.

Why can't we have it all now? We have too much of this world in us to handle the Infinite. Now we are in a time of development, of spiritual growth, of laying aside the lesser darkness in order to attain new vistas of life. We learn to joy in the learning process, even to be thankful for the necessary pruning we at times need. Now we are Becomers, pilgrims upon the blessed road of resurrections and renewals. Now we are in a time of shedding, of laying aside the lesser for the greater. We are fellow sojourners living out God's covenant with Abraham and Sarah.

The stewardship of our physical bodies

There is another dimension to all of this. That light energy of love flowing into our spiritual essence also flows into our body. Years of behavior patterns, which we have labeled as sin, have crippled our body, curtailing its functions. We have mind sets and attitudes which have weakened our body and shortened our very life span. To a degree we will allow it, because of our spiritual resurrection, there is a new power working in our physical body. As the Holy Paraclete is allowed to do its work, more of the light love energy becomes available for daily living.

Here we must address an attitude that can be so crippling, the attitude we have toward our own physical body. We need to remember that when God made this creation He pronounced it good, not just once, but seven times, ending, after He had made humans, by saying it is very good. (Genesis 1:31) Sometimes we take Paul too literally when he said our physical bodies are "a body of death." (Romans 7:24)

Our physical bodies are but a container, a vehicle, housing our spiritual essence. Our physical makeup is crowned with a mind, an executive ego, which makes its choices based upon our attitudes, mind sets, emotions and our belief system. Our attitudes guide our executive ego into determining what our body will do and become. Too often we have an adversarial relationship with our physical body.

If we are obese it is not the fault of our body, it is our attitudes which lead to the choices which made our body obese. So it is with sexual desires, stress-related tensions that wreck our bodies, fears that shorten our life, angers that drain the energy from our bodies and feelings of worthlessness that lead to all kinds of physical reactions. The condition of our bodies is directly related to our attitudes.

When our attitudes are rebuilt by our indwelling Holy Spirit into positive factors, our body, including our mind and our emotions, can then receive the light energy of love reinforcement needed for good health. Key to remember, our bodies are not our adversaries, they simply reflect our attitudes, mind sets, emotions and belief systems. They are a physical expression of the choices we have made!

This includes the sexual dimension of our lives. At our creation God pronounced our human creation very good. (Genesis 1:31) Affirmation according to the Will is the path of life. Negation of goodness for the sake of achieving greater holiness is not the Will of God!

Our Creator saw fit to build into our bodies five sensory receptors: sight, sound, taste, scent and touch, which if guided rightly, are designed to protect us and lend pleasure to our living. Both our spirit and our flesh are designed to "sing for joy to the living God." (Psalm 84:2) There is to be a harmony, best expressed by the Greek "golden mean," between our emotions, our mental abilities, our physical body and our spiritual essence. Since everyone is different, no formula will work for everyone. As we journey with our Good Shepherd we will find that harmony for the uniquely me.

When we have a physical problem we need to look to the attitudes which contributed to the problem. It is no accident that the New Testament begins with the only sermon we have of Jesus and that begins with eight blessed attitudes, the Beatitudes.

Jesus never promised us physical healing. Too many times we need our aches and pains to show us a need for a stronger love-bond with our Savior. Pains are designed to be heralds of problems! But the Jesus Way of Life is a positive attitude; which helps us deal with our aches and pains. Realistic attitudes help us take better care of our physical body. They tell us of behavior patterns that need changing. Through paying attention to them, the quality of our lives, as we live it out in our physical bodies, can not only be improved but lead to many moments upon mountains designed by our Creator.

A word of caution! Just as Jesus and all of us face that temptation to focus on the physical bread of life rather than feeding our spiritual essence, we can so focus on the aches and pains of our physical body that there is no time for the spiritual love bond to develop. We are spiritual beings *temporarily* here in a physical body.

This temporary time in our body is filled with stress, depressions, angers, addictions and lusts. Learning to develop the fruit of the Holy Spirit: love, joy, peace, patience, kindness, goodness, faithfulness, gentleness and self-discipline (Galatians 5:22), allows the healing properties of the love light energy to flow through our bodies, targeting various needs, with its healing properties. The results are amazing.

Life is to be a growing experience. Too often we seek to control our behavior via our mind and will. It is sometimes very difficult for us to "let go and let God!" As we do so, as we allow the Spirit of Truth and Love to take more and more control of our behavior, both spiritually and physically, we will experience vistas of spiritual beauty undreamed of at the beginning of our life's journey. Since we will one day be only a spiritual entity, why not get used to the idea! Why not discover what it is to journey with the Holy Spirit rather than consulting Him from time to time when we feel a need!

This journey of increased awareness is very personal. Each of us has a special one-on-one relationship with Jesus through the Spirit that is Holy that dwells within us and is connected to the Zero Point Field. This relationship is designed to grow into a love bond. Each follower has a special love name given by Jesus. (John 10:3, 4) Each of us is a special gem stone capable of reflecting and refracting the light energy of love in our own special way, as in the vision of the New Jerusalem in the book of Revelation. (21:19)

Ignoring spiritual realities

There are many ways and means whereby we can avoid dealing with the spiritual dimension of our lives. Too many times modern doctors and psychologists attempt to improve healing with a total focus on the physical. Let's not follow that deviant path. The arguments over Gestalt psychology, of the need to include the spiritual if complete healing is to be attained, are part of history. We are spiritual beings temporarily here in a physical body and to ignore that spiritual dimension personifies foolishness!

To live in harmony with the Natural Laws which govern this creation and our very selves is not a new idea. It is the basis of eastern healing. Since sin not only destroys our soul but cripples our body, why not live in harmony with the forces of life within and about us?

We can ignore the spiritual dimension in other ways: We can focus upon industrial wastes polluting our island home. We can focus upon the folly of making government the new messiah, capable of solving all our problems. We can focus upon programs which make money but ignore the harm they do to humans. It seems that the banking and merchant industries will justify any and all situations via the "bottom line!" We can focus upon religions that encourage killing all unbelievers! We can focus on the wars, the killings that are part of wars and the destruction caused by wars. It is alluring to fixate on deviant behavior but avoid dealing with the spiritual dimension which caused the behavior! Such fixations can demonstrates our moral superiority, giving us a cause that makes us feel good! But is a feeling of moral superiority the the goal of our moral sensibilities? Emphatically not!

Human problems are created by lives focused upon the ways and means of the world, taking care of number one, seeking the pleasures of life through the senses, assuming that the lust of the eyes and the vainglory of life is what life is all about. We humans have made our societies and our personal living what they are—so much less than they could and should be. Who's fault is it? Who must change to improve it?

Our critics ask, "Why doesn't a God of love fix our human messes?" HE HAS! He has shown us how to live in the Natural Law. He has shown us the love foundation needed to live well during our brief time while in our physical body. He has placed the Holy Spirit in the unconscious of every human. He has provided the ministering Angels. He has given us human history. What more could He do? Do the work of changing this world _for_ us? Never! We have the tools. It is stated in the Bible as the Rainbow Covenant given to us in that teaching story about Noah and the Ark. (Genesis 9:8-17)

God will not destroy errant humans and start over again. We are here; we are "it."

As Jesus told His disciples, whomever we lose from their sins on earth through the Jesus Way of Life through Love will be forever released, whoever is not released to walk the Jesus Way is not going to be released by angels! (Matthew 18:18, John 20:23) As His name states, Yahweh Jireh, the God Who Provides, has provided the way, the means and the empowerment we need. Our very spiritual development depends upon our being a witness of God's Way of Life through love—being light and salt. Whatever happens in human history happens by human choices, not by God not caring. He went to the cross in shameful death to open the Way. If we don't walk it, it is by our choices, not God's!

The Creator's Plan of salvation through Jesus

In spite of all human behavior, there is always the Creator's Plan of salvation for those who will walk it. In spite of all we humans have done, the Jesus Way of Life through love never fails. It is an existential reality—it works. It has always worked. It is the reason why so many would rather sacrifice their physical body than give up this love-bonded relationship with Jesus once they recognize they are a part of the blessed Gospel Covenant. Those without this experience will never understand it. The evil one has the ability to present many reasons why it is all nonsense. Too many will reject God's plan as nonsense and choose to believe instead, in a nothingness.

This is all in the Bible if one knows how to read the Bible. For any humble seeker who will quietly come into harmony with the stillness, the faith and the trust in the Holy Spirit, passages from the Bible will become life-affirming messages of truth. Don't try to explain this to the non-followers, they won't get it and won't believe it. Unbelief engenders more unbelief. Trust and obey, seek and we will find, knock and it will be opened to us, Jesus said. (Matthew 7:7) Every follower of Jesus knows the truth of that promise.

But let's not argue over the validity of various sacred scriptures. Let's go to the spiritual realities from which various authors of religious scriptures, especially the authors of the Bible, have derived their understandings. Let's go to the realities which existed before anything was written, and exists in its full glory for any who will walk that path today and will exist long after the human race has chosen to extinguish itself!

Life's basic reality

We come back to the basic reality: we are spiritual beings existing temporarily in a physical body. We have our desires for beauty, love, truth and the goodness in this creation. We know our problems of sin. There is a way provided by which we can turn the past pages of our less-than-perfect living, old cycles which need rejection so new cycles become possible, patterns of behavior which are less crippled by sin's legacy. Through Jesus we can live in harmony with our loving Father in the Existential Now, the only reality we can ever truly know.

We can learn from our mistakes. But, especially, we can learn from what works, our moments of achievement, our moment on the mountain with Jesus. We can learn how to use the light energy of love from the Source in our everyday living. We can become accustomed to the presence of not just evil with its temptations, but of the Holy Angels and their ministrations. We can allow the Spirit that is Holy to guide and empower us for abundant living. We can learn how to use the light, love, life energy of God's Will in our choice-making. We can learn to bend our fallible will to the Infallible Infinite and learn how to truly live. We can learn how to reach beyond the physical into the spiritual dimensions available for our living. We can learn how to make Jesus and His life and teachings central to our lives. We can journey in the Spirit into amazing new vistas, new insights and new possibilities. We can learn to let go and let God!

Sure, we will make mistakes, wonder off the Narrow Way at times, but our Heavenly Shepherd will always come to us with guidance and empowerment for resurrected living. We can learn to use the Five R's of repentance: Recognizing our mistakes, Repenting, saying we are sorry, Rejecting the behavior, Remembering our Higher Power for strength to change and then Rebuild our lives in new and better ways.

Our new citizenship

A Jewish religious leader, Nicodemus, came to Jesus by night, so he wouldn't be seen, to speak with Jesus as a teacher of special insights. (John 3:1f) Jesus cut short all discussions with the simple statement translated in English as "You must be born from above." This born from above, or as it is sometimes translated, "born again," has given us some wrong insights into this new life of which Jesus spoke.

The Greek word is not "genesis" but "genao." "Genesis" speaks of physical birth, a happening. "Genao" means a new citizenship, a new relationship. The book of Revelation speaks of "they who dwell in Heaven," as over against "they who dwell on earth." (Revelation 13:6-8) Jesus called it they who have entered the narrow gate and are traveling on the Narrow Way which leads to life as different from those who walk the Broad Highway leading to destruction. (Matthew 7:13, 14) When interrogated by Pilate, the Roman governor, Jesus said He was a king in the Kingdom of Truth. (John 18:36, 37) We are either part of God's Plan for our salvation or we remain in some human idea of what we need to do to get what we want out of life. We must allow ourselves to continually grow in our spiritual citizenship or we will drift out of the Father's hand. (John 10:29) No one or nothing can snatch us out of His blessed hand, but we can drift out, as the second and third plants did in the Parable of the Sower, (Matthew 13:1f)

The Father's offer

Our Heavenly Father offers us a life of adventure, of leaving the lesser for the greater. This invitation will never change. Life is designed to be a journey with Jesus, our Good Shepherd, with the Holy Spirit, with the Holy Angels under the sheltering wings of the Heavenly Father. (Psalm 91) There can be no greater adventure. And we can experience this reality even though we cannot imagine what and where this adventure will take us but we will love and enjoy the trip as we allow the spiritual love-based life to change and develop us into our new citizenship, our new Gospel Covenant relationship!

The omnipotent power is the Sustainer's Will, the light of love. We are to utilize that power by deriving energy for living from it.

It all begins by accepting by faith the gift of Jesus—forgiveness for our sins through His death on Calvary. We are justified, made members of Jesus' kingdom of truth by that faith. Then we begin the life-long process of sanctification—learning how to love as Jesus loved and loves us, of being led by the Spirit rather than the flesh. By so doing we are exercising our new citizenship. We are part of the Kingdom of God on earth and especially in Heaven. This is our Promised Land of the Plan of God.

Now what are we, what am I, going to do about it? Will I allow myself to grow into a precious stone in the new Jerusalem by reflecting and refracting the glory of His Message, His sacrifice? (Revelation 21:9-27) Or will I allow myself to drift with "the cowardly and the unbelieving and the abominable and murderers and immoral persons and sorcerers and idolaters and all liars. Their part will be in the lake that burns with fire and brimstone, which is the second death." (Revelation 21:8)

A Meditation

Blessed Heavenly Father, Lord Jesus, Holy Spirit
    How can I ever thank You enough for this plan of salvation?
What You ask of me is so simple
    Just be a part of all this eternal preparation and revelation
        Commit to it
Experience the glory of Your Will in the order and harmony of Natural Law
    Allow the light energy of love of Your Will to flow into my soul
        Remove the obstacles which still restrict the flow
            Through Your divine umbilical cord of light and love
Experience the fellowship with Jesus
    Listening and obeying His teachings
        Living resurrected lives because of His death on Calvary
            Learning to become His friend in this journey of life
Experience the love of the Spirit that is Holy
    Listening to its guidance
        Accepting and using its power for resurrected living
Enjoy the fellowship of the Holy Angels
    Fellow servants of mine who have already undergone the winnowing
        Have already chosen the way of life through love
        And can minister that love to me
That I may live well in the existential nows of my life
    Choosing moment by moment to allow Your Will into my heart
        Laying aside the lesser for the larger
            Opening to new vistas of Your light and life
So shall I ever thank You for what You have provided for me

So shall I find that special place You have prepared for me.
All I need to do is look to You in gratitude
    And pray from my heart
        "Yes, Lord, whatever it is, yes!"
I pray for the strength and the commitment
    That I may follow You
        To the green pastures and still waters of life.
    So I will find the life You have prepared for me
Not just for a generic us, Your followers
    But You know my name
I am part of a special, personal love bond
    You have designed and prepared for me
I can learn how to refract and reflect the light of life
    In a way only I can do it.

CHAPTER FIVE

Living in the Anteroom of Life

What a Plan of salvation, of gracious living, of beautiful potential, our Heavenly Father has prepared for us! What power, what prospects await us in every existential now of our living through the light energy of love He desires to pour into our being! Why isn't this world singing for joy for the love that would liberate all peoples, all nations and especially every individual, and form them into a fellowship of perfect harmony? What went wrong? Why doesn't everyone elect to live this life?

We could spend hours commiserating over the faults, the corruption and the prevalent evil in human affairs besmirching this beautiful planet Earth. And our human mess is most damnably real! We must never hide our heads from such realities in ostrich-like behavior. But neither must we continually focus on what is wrong, for there is so much more that is right. It is in order to bring into being what is so right, what can be so right, that God brought His Plan for our salvation into being and sustains it through His holy Will.

What went wrong? We focused our living on the wrong thing! We fixated on the ways and means of those who have not chosen to be led by the Spirit that is Holy. We who were designed to become beings capable of living in the Spiritual World for eternity traded this potential for a little more physical comfort, things, and ease of living!

The miracle of it all is that we fallible human beings, we vessels of clay that at birth know little more than how to nurse, can be part of our Creator's holy Plan, initiated by His grace and sustained by His love. Even while our body ages we can grow and develop into spiritual beings akin to the angels. We are finite beings designed to live for a cycle of existence in a physical body, existing within the Infinitude of love and power of His Holy Will. To exist in that Infinitude we need to allow it to do its Will in us, help us to develop into spiritual beings capable of making that journey into Infinity after the death of our physical bodies!

And the glory of it all is that we can experience all this while living in our physical bodies, in this vessel of clay that contains for a while our spiritual essence, the real me. Of a certainty this earthen vessel is weak, encumbered with ideas that don't work, with a genetic code we did not choose, with our physical characteristics, even our sex, not of our choosing. But it is ours, mine, and I will have no other. We are wedded together for a while, this physical entity and my spiritual essence.

The amazing beauty of it all is that by the grace and empowerment of my indwelling Holy Paraclete, I can grow up spiritually through this daily interaction with the physical. Together we can turn the physical pain, the ignorance, the tragedies and the shortcomings into spiritual growth! Amazing! Mind boggling! Our bodies are not evil. They are a stewardship we have been given for our spiritual development.

We will live out our cycle of life in the anteroom of eternity. Just beyond our last breath, our last heart-beat, is the Spiritual World, which the spiritual Me, the real Me, has so long sought to engage in a more perfect unity. Our longing for the fruit of the work of the Holy Spirit: love, joy, peace, patience, kindness, goodness, faithfulness, gentleness and self-discipline, will finally reach its full potential.

The key to this divine program is not denial but affirmation, turning the experiences of living into spiritual development. Through the work of the Spirit that is Holy we can learn how to follow our Good Shepherd. Jesus said He was the Bread of Life (John 6:35), the Light of the World (John 8:12), the Door of the Sheepfold (John 10:9), the Good Shepherd (John 10:14), Resurrection and Life (11:25), the Way and the Truth and the Life (John 14:6) and the Vine of spiritual growth through the spiritual sustenance arising from the root, the umbilical cord of life which is Jesus (John 15:1-12).

We are learning to accept the Jesus invitation to real life. Everyone has their own personal spiritual experiences. The glory of our personal spiritual encounters reaches beyond the immediate, the particular, to as much joy as we are able to incorporate into our living, given our attitudes, our mind sets and our faith.

Scoffers will say, "What if it isn't true? Then all your work turns out for nothing!"

Not for nothing! We have had the most glorious experiences while learning what we most wanted: how to experience love, find joy, experience peace in the midst of disasters, develop patience in life's living, experience the joy of kindnesses, goodness, faithfulness and gentleness, through learning how to develop spiritual order through self-discipline. In Jesus we have learned and experienced something of what we truly want, the Jesus Way of Life through love.

We are experiencing an awareness of so much we never guessed in our wildest imagination. To feel the unity of it all through what we now call the Zero Point Field, to grasp something of the spiritual dimension of life, to recognize something of the love of God for our living, to see vistas of beauty and truth and to be a part of it all, has answered the questions of the "why" and the "what" of our existence, of my existence.

Skeptics will go through their cycle of living without finding the fruit of the spiritual dimension, however limited we may experience it in this life. They have simply denied themselves the most glorious of life's adventures! Life is so much more than the sum of the parts of our physical bodies, ask anyone who is walking the Narrow Way of life by following our Good Shepherd.

The invitation

As a human being, we can choose to be a part of it or ignore it or even reject it! Jesus stands at our soul's door every day seeking entrance into something new, something more vast, a spiritual something we don't even know exists except by faith. Again, the miracle of it all is that we can be a part of it by simply allowing it to happen; by removing the obstacles which keep that door locked and by allowing ourselves to cross the faith bridge!

The conclusion

We have come to share a fellowship as we have meditated on the truths, the revelations which God has opened before us. We are one in the schema of life, the Will of our creator.

My wife Iris and I have worked together with members of our Christian Fellowship to put this love letter together. We are the First Century Christian Fellowship of Lindale, Texas. We are associated with Lutheran Congregations in Mission for Christ, but don't allow that to disturb you.

If you will turn to the beautiful seventh chapter of Revelation you will read of the twelve tribes before the Throne. Twelve is the family number in the Bible. These "twelve" tribes are the family of Christ. Some of the "family" are Orthodox, some Roman Catholic, some Presbyterian and so on. We are all committed to following the Good Shepherd and learning how to love one another as He loved us, even if we have different traditions for so doing. Every follower of the Jesus Way of Life through love is part of that vast assemblage, the one universal family, the one catholic entity.

Sometimes we need to turn to that last parable of Jesus; the one about the sheep and the goats and the final judgment. (Matthew 25:312f) This is Jesus telling us the criteria of the final judgment, the criteria by which every human will be evaluated. Not what group did you belong, what theology did you learn and teach, but did you feed the hungry, clothe the naked, visit the sick and the lonely, set prisoners free, both spiritually and physically? To "know" Jesus is to walk His Way.

Is this work perfect? Of course not! Nothing human is ever perfect or finished. But may the truth be a blessing and what is not be forgiven in Christ's Holy Name. You may want to remove the "I" and put your name in the following confession as I summarize the witness of the Spirit that is Holy in our lives, in my life.

A Confession

I possess a spiritual essence living for a period of time and place in my physical body. This vessel has a genetic foundation I did not choose. I was born into a family, a sex, with physical characteristics and a set of childhood experiences, most of which I did not choose. I developed a set of attitudes, most of which I absorbed from my parents and other teachers and friends during my childhood experiences. But I am here in this, my Existential Now, the only moment in my living I will dependably have. So what will I do with what I have in this moment in time, for I am more than a corpse, dead tissue? I have, for the moment, life and the ability through the Holy Spirit to choose more life!

There is an angry, self-pitying side of my consciousness infected with plom's disease (poor little old me)! I can look at the world around me and within me and see the usual mess. But at this existential moment of my life I do not choose to be mesmerized by the darkness. I do not excuse the evil nor hide from it. I simply do not choose to allow the works of evil to be the focus of my life.

I want love, beauty, peace, joy and goodness, not just in theory, but in the daily living of my life by means of whatever I can do to make that a part of my life. I choose to so work that God's Kingdom may come and His Will be done within me and become part of that which exists around me. For inspiration I can find in the living world around me, in the plants, animals and birds of this creation, in the glory of their cycles of living, a harmony with that which I seek. I find in the life and teachings of Jesus the same mighty witness of the good and the beautiful, coupled with the simple fact that He is my

Savior who went to that shameful death for me when He took the consequences of my sins upon Himself.

Wishful thinking? It is my experience in my daily living! It works! *Faith* in that reality sets me free to learn how to walk the Way of Life through love. Through God's *grace,* His love for me, change, new beginnings, resurrected living, are not only possible, but are realities upon which I can learn how to walk the path of love-based spiritual growth. In Him is life and grace and the Holy *Word* I need for living.

I do not and will not hide from the reality that there is also a mess within me. I am aware of attitudes, of reactions, of temptations and moods less that what they should be. I do mourn for what is not but should and could be. I do hunger and thirst for righteousness, beginning with what I can do and be at this moment, in order to make my life more in harmony with the Will that sustains me. I am beginning to realize how the joys of the Lord can be my strength.

I am trying to walk the Way of Life Jesus outlined for Peter. (John 21:15-17) I do love the ways and spiritual things of Jesus more than anything else. I am committing to learning how to make love the foundation for my life. I am discovering what it means to have Jesus as my dearest friend; One who knows me, understands all my struggles and problems; the One who loves me, warts and all, and will never abandon me! Who walks with me day by day.

This is my faith; but it is more than just a trust, it is a way I am trying to live my life. I am aware of energy centers about and within me, the Holy Spirit and the angelic presences. I am also aware of the dark presences of evil. When I open up to the light energy of love, the Will of the Father, my energy field expands and begins to fill the space within and about me. I am part of so much more, such interconnected harmony, such beauty, that, even while I stand in awe of it all, I desire more at whatever the cost.

This sharpens the focus of my struggles, for I am no plaster saint. I struggle with the lesser that too often refuses to develop and grow. But in the midst of it all, the Spirit that is Holy has shown me the key to living well—opening to God's surrounding Will, removing the obstacles, allowing my spiritual essence to grow and develop!

I have learned of His plan for the human race: The Law Covenant, His covenant with Abraham and Sarah, which is my covenant, my need for a Savior, the Gospel Covenant of my new relationship with God, my membership in His Kingdom and the special place Jesus has prepared for me in eternity for my developing spiritual essence after I lay aside my body.

I commit to that truth and find in that commitment the power of light, of love and life, enter my being as I allow it entrance, daily, hourly, for my spiritual development, but also spilling over into the stewardship of my physical body. My life grows as it focuses upon the spiritual, the light energy of life and the discipline of righteous choices, during this my time in this anteroom, before my entrance into eternity. Jesus is the central focus of my life and living. I am His bond servant by choice.

This is the conclusion of my love note which I wish to share with my sisters and brothers, the fellowship of the members of the journey, the ancient Way. I am so grateful for each fellow traveler though we may be separated by time, space and ideologies. As part of the Zero Point Field, the Tribal Unconscious, we are a family, each of us reflecting and refracting the glory of God in our own way, as in that vision of the New Jerusalem at the end of the book of Revelation. We are one flock in one pasture. I am I and you are you and we are all each other too. In Jesus Holy Name! Amen.

May we together open ourselves to the love of the Father, the fellowship of Jesus, the guidance and empowerment of the Holy Spirit and the ministry of the Holy Angels as they seek to envelop and unite us at this moment of our living into a harmony with the Eternal Plan based upon Natural Law, through the avenues of the Zero Point Field, all within the Holy Will of love which sustains and supports us, now and for all eternity. Amen

APPENDIX ONE

God's Grand Plan—The Holy Seven

The inside of the divine is always so much greater and glorious than the outside! As we survey the Plan of God, what He has revealed to us as the purpose, the teleological end of what our Heavenly Creator has done for us, the holy number seven comes into focus. The number seven was regarded as holy because it illustrates a wholeness possible through the unity of the divine three and the earthly four.

The Holy Trinity, the divine three, consists of the revelations of the <u>Father</u> in creation, <u>Jesus</u> in His teachings and His life-giving sacrifice as the Lamb of God taking away the sins of the world and the <u>Spirit that is Holy</u>, the Holy Paraclete, indwelling our unconscious but rising into our consciousness with the guidance and empowerment we need for spiritual growth and development.

The earthly four are the four dimensions our love must have if we are to learn how to love as Jesus loves us. Those dimensions are our relationship with <u>God</u>, with <u>ourselves</u>, with <u>others</u> and with the rest of this <u>creation</u>.

Given the needs of we human beings and the wishes of a Deity of love, the fantastic unity, symphony and harmony of it all grows with the distance one journeys following our Good Shepherd on the Narrow Way of life through love. Let us begin where we must begin if we would grasp anything of the glory of it all, with our needed love-bond with the Holy Trinity which created, redeemed and guides and empowers us for living in this creation in which we find ourselves.

The Divine Trinity:

This earth is a perfect home for us. It has the right inclination on its axis to provide the needed seasons, the right amount of water to purify the atmosphere and provide the balance needed through the ratio of water to land. It is the right distance from our star, the sun. Earth has been in existence long enough to provide the needed carbon-based energy sources, oil and coal. Organisms needed to develop hematite developed so iron became possible. The time signatures of rotation on earth's axis and revolutions around the sun are neither too long nor too short.

This list could go on for many pages, all signifying the perfect planet for the existence of a being capable of learning, of loving and of understanding something of the meaning of it all as the Spirit that is Holy imparts the wisdom.

When we didn't "get it," <u>God the Father</u> gave us a simplified version of Natural Law in the Ten Commandments. When we had trouble "getting" the larger meaning, a divine Messenger, <u>God the Son</u>, came from Heaven to live as a human and to not only teach us what we needed to know, illustrate it by His life, give us the ultimate love commandment and then become the substitutionary atonement for our sins as the sacrificial Lamb of God. To make sure we had what we need to understand our reason for existence, our goal in life and how to reach that goal, <u>God the Holy Spirit</u> came to indwell our unconscious.

Our Creator and Sustainer, our Teacher and Redeemer, our Guide and Empowerment for living, have provided all we need to know and the empowerment we need to live well on this special island home so perfectly fitted to our needs. What about the human four?

The Human Four:

God is love and He illustrates that love by caring for this creation, including us, responding to our real needs, respecting the integrity of each element of this creation and understanding us, our definition of love. In order for us to live well during the cycle of our existence upon this planet, we need to learn how to love. It was the commandment of Jesus—love one another as I have loved you; by this all mankind will know you are My disciples. (John 13:34, 35, 15:12, 17) That love is to be expressed in four relationships: in a love-bond with God, with ourselves, with others and with the rest of this creation.

Learning to love God

The history of human religions illustrate a development from sacrifices to please what is considered a deity, to a recognition of the laws of this creation and the need to live in harmony with the Deity who made it, to a need to learn how to base that obedience upon a love-bond, to making that love-bond a personal commitment. As Jesus stated it, we learn to love Him more than anything else, we are to base our human relationships upon love and we are to develop a personal friendship-bond with Jesus. (John 21:15-17) Since it is the light energy of love which built and now sustains this creation, we must learn how to love if we are going to be a part of it!

Learning to love ourselves

Loving ourselves can be quite a problem. We came into existence with a set of genes, characteristics and relationships of which we had no choice. Can we learn to respect and learn how to positively use what we have been given? To love oneself is not a problem of selfishness as long as the other three loves are also part of our living: loving the Deity, others and the rest of this creation. Each of us is a unique and special individual. Learning how to properly care for, respond to our real needs, respect our individuality and understand our life's situations will certainly take a lifetime, but if we don't begin the process we cannot truly love anything else!

Loving others

Loving others is again to carry out the formula of caring, meeting needs, respecting the other and learning to understand life's situations. We extend ourselves for the spiritual welfare of others. We learn how to exercise proper judgment in the forgiveness of the person committing injustices while identifying their sins as being sins! We are to be merciful if we wish to obtain mercy. (Matthew 5:7) Loving others in such a manner that does not build dependency but builds love-based spiritual relationships is key to it all. As with all our love relationships, this is a life-long process.

Learning to love our natural environment

Learning to love our natural environment is designed to be key to getting to know who and what we are. Having the humility, the curiosity and the willingness to bond to the natural elements of this creation, plus spending the time to absorb the music, the harmonies and the relationships of the grand symphony of it all, guarantees a refreshing of our spirit. We who must choose our allegiance to Natural Law as a basis of our well being, find personal refreshment in those elements which are, have been and always will be faithful to their Creator.

The umbilical cord of love

The bond of love is the umbilical cord uniting the Divine Three and the Earthly Four. Our personal human welfare is built upon the flowage of that love light energy from the Source into our soul.

God has provided, now it is we who are to be the light and salt of this world into which we find ourselves or there will be no light or salt! Our personal well being is dependent upon how we allow that divine energy flow to be transmitted through ourselves into the world around us. Each of us has a measurable aura. The extension of that aura is based upon the love energy flowage through us.

The Parable of the Sheep and the Goats

Judging the ability of any soul to function in a Spiritual World after laying aside their physical body is based upon how well they have exercised their love development while in their physical body. As in the Parable of the Sheep and the Goats (Matthew 25:31f), every human must, of necessity, be evaluated by how well they have built love bonds by feeding the hungry, clothing the naked, visiting the lonely, the sick and the stranger and did they set the imprisoned free—spiritually and physically? What else could prepare us for living in a love-based Spiritual World?

The sin obstacle

The great obstacle is our sin. Once any human committed an act of rebellion, any sinful act, they became a sinner, incapable of being part of the Spiritual World. Imperfections must not be allowed in the perfect world or it is no longer perfect! A way must be found whereby sinful humans could be reinstated into their sinless state if they were to be allowed in the Spiritual World. Enter the substitutionary atonement idea. Someone living had to take the consequences of human sin upon themselves. Animals couldn't do it for humans—they were not of the same status. Enter a human substitute for human sin.

The Jesus solution

But although one human could die for another, there are no perfect humans; each must be punished for their own sins! Enter the divine Jesus who was also a human being—the perfect substitute for our sins. So the historical Jesus, with the historical prerequisites did the historical act. Then He arose from the dead to appear to His followers then and down through the ages. As He told His disciples, "In a little while the world will see Me no more, but you will see Me, because I live, you will live also." (John 14:19)

The Salvation Message

This is the message the Holy Spirit tries to impart into the consciousness of every person: The Way of Life through love. Those who elect to follow this pathway of life, learning to love God, themselves, others and the rest of this creation, experience the spiritual connectedness, the spiritual bonding of love, even if they have never heard of the name of Jesus. As Jesus said, "They will come from the east and the west and recline at table with Abraham and Isaac and Jacob in the kingdom of heaven." (Matthew 8:11)

This is God's Plan, which is supported by His Will extending into the soul of every human. No human is exempt—being too sinful or not being very sinful. But each must elect to walk the spiritual Way of Life through love. To remain as part of the world of sinners, worldly attitudes and soul destructive behavior patterns guarantees a total wastage of the opportunity God gives everyone to become an eternal entity existing for all eternity. It is our faith in the Jesus atonement, our faith in the walk of learning how to love, which makes us whole, which fulfills our Father's love-based plan for our salvation.

APPENDIX TWO

Miscellaneous Listings

The Ten Commandments (Exodus 20:1-17, Deuteronomy 5:6-21)

Table One

1. You shall have no other Gods but Me
2. You shall not make an idol or any likeness of what is in heaven above or on earth beneath or in the waters under the earth.
3. You shall not take the Name of the Lord your God in vain.
4. Remember the Sabbath Day and keep it holy.
5. Honor your father and mother that your days may be long upon the land which the Lord your God gives you.

Table Two

6. You shall do no murder.
7. You shall not commit adultery.
8. You shall not steal.
9. You shall not bear false witness.
10. You shall not covet your neighbor's house nor his wife nor his property nor anything that belongs to your neighbor.

Remember these had to be brief as they were chiseled on tablets of stone the size of which Moses could carry!

Seven vicissitudes of Life:

1. The mistakes of others which affect me
2. My mistakes which affect others and myself
3. My ignorance
4. My illnesses
5. My personal and natural catastrophes
6. The aging process
7. Active evil

The Five R's of Repentance

1. Recognition of a sin
2. Repenting, saying we are sorry
3. Rejecting the behavior
4. Remembering our Higher Power for strength to change
5. Rebuilding our lives in a new a better way

The Six Stages of sin

1. Awareness of the forbidden
2. Listening to the temptation
3. The first lie, it would be good for you
4. The second lie, God won't punish you
5. Doing it
6. Getting others to participate

The Five Imperatives of Jesus

1. Love one another as I have loved you (John 13:34, 15:12, 17)
2. You shall be perfect as the Heavenly Father is perfect (Matthew 5:48)
3. You shall as merciful as the Heavenly Father is merciful (Luke 6:36)

4. You shall seek first the Kingdom of God and His righteousness (Matthew 6:33)
5. You shall love your enemies and pray for them (Matthew 5:44)

The Seven I Am's of Jesus in the Gospel of John

1. "I am the bread of life, they who come to me will never hunger, they who believe in Me will never thirst." (John 6:35)
2. "I am the light of the world, they who follow after Me shall not walk in darkness but shall have the light of life." (John 8:12)
3. "I am the door, if anyone enters through Me, he shall go in and out and find pasture. The thief comes to steal and kill and destroy, I come that you may have life and have it more abundantly." (John 10:9, 10)
4. "I am the good Shepherd, and I know My own and My own know Me…and I lay down My life for the sheep." (John 10:14, 15)
5. "I am the resurrection and the life, they who believe in Me shall live even if they die, and everyone who lives and believes in Me shall never die." (John 11:25, 26)
6. "I am the way and the truth and the life, no one comes to the Father except through Me." (John 14:5)
7. "I am the true vine, and My Father is the vine dresser. Every branch that does not bear fruit He takes away, and every branch that bears fruit He prunes that it may bear more fruit." John 15:1, 2)

The Seven I Am's of Jesus in the book of Revelation

1. "I am the Alpha and the Omega, who is and who was and who is to come, the Almighty." (Revelation 1:8)

2. "I am the first and the last and the living One, I was dead, and behold, I am alive forevermore and I have the keys of death and Hades." (Revelation 1:17, 18)
3. "I am He who searches the minds and the hearts, and I will give to each one of you according to your deeds." (Revelation 2:23)
4. "I am the Alpha and the Omega, the beginning and the end." (Revelation 21:6)
5. "I am the Alpha and the Omega, the first and the last, the beginning and the end." (Revelation 22:13)
6. "I am the root and the offspring of David." (Revelation 22:16)
7. "I am…the bright and morning star." (Revelation 22:16)

Four Perspectives for Viewing the Bible

1. It is good Literature, such as Shakespeare or Tolstoy
2. It is literally, word for word, the Word of God
3. It is God's revelation of His truth spoken through human agents
4. It is God's revelation of His truth spoken through human hands designed to lead us to Jesus as understood in the First Century.

Kant's categorical Imperative:

What if everybody did it? What kind of society would result? What if murder were the accepted means of settling disputes. What if there were no marriage vows as a foundation for a family? What if theft was accepted human behavior? What if the lie were the standard of communication rather than the truth. What if everyone took what they wanted from anyone they had the strength to overpower?

Through a long and difficult struggle we have learned the value of the five commandments of the second table. Human civilization rests upon these five statements from Natural Law: You shall do no murder, commit adultery, steal, lie, or covet what is another's. In Jesus Christ the ethic of the Commandments are joined to the love motivation for fulfilling the Commandments. The ethical standard needed for human living is a perfectly unity of the spiritual Trinity with the needs of human living.

That Third temptation:

Will we commit to God's Kingdom or remaining in the ways and means of the physical world? Every living human is born into this world with the folkways and mores of families and larger social entities. Every human is like every other human with the needs for food, shelter and clothing, plus a little pleasure! Every human will pursue what they think will get them what they consider their needs for living.

But every human is given a desire for something more, some ideal, something spiritually satisfying, something often unnamed but real. That hunger for righteousness can be blunted by alcohol, drugs, immoral behavior or or various physical goals. NOTHING WILL SATISFY THAT DRIVE BUT THE WAY OF LIFE THROUGH LOVE AS LIVED AND TAUGHT BY JESUS.

The great question with which every human must deal is simple: The Way of Life through love as actuated by the love energy of the Will, or going our own headstrong way? WE ARE GOING OUR OWN WAY unless we choose again and again to go God's Way. That Way is opened for us through learning how to love God, ourselves, others and the rest of this creation—that greatest of human needs—love. No one is exempt from this invitation. Oddly enough, it is those who are obvious sinners, obviously in need of a new pathway of living, who will sometimes elect to walk the Jesus Way. It is the self-righteous, those who have seeming moral credentials, that are the most resistant to this invitation. We must never mistake the invitation: God so loved the world that He gave His only begotten son that whosoever would believe in Him may have eternal life, for

God sent not His Son into the world to condemn the world but that the world through Him might be saved." (John 3:16, 17)

A Meditation

Out of the unknown and the unfathomable
    I am
I did not choose my existence
    But I am none-the-less here
And I have those eternal questions before me:
        The spiritual or only the material?
        The Will of the Source, my Creator, or my will?
        Choosing the Kingdom of God
            Or remaining in the ways of the world?
I recognize the simple fact
    I am under the Iron Law of Jesus
        I will become what I choose
    This day and for all eternity!
I am not capable of dealing with such awesome choices
    I need a Savior
    An indwelling Holy Paraclete
    The ministrations of the Holy Angels
    The history of those who lived before me
I need a loving Heavenly Father Who will Provide for me
    And I need to commit to those provisions
I do not choose to be an orphan
    I will open the door of my heart to Jesus
I commit to allowing the love light energy of Your Will, my Father
    To replace my personal darkness
Lord, I want what You have to offer
    I want to learn how to love as Jesus loves me
    I want to learn to be as merciful as You are merciful
    I want to learn how to love those who trouble me
    I want to more fully place the ways of Your Kingdom first

I want to be in perfect harmony
> With the Natural Laws which order my existence

And so I come to You at this special moment
> This personal existential moment of this cycle of my life
>> Balanced between a past and a future

I am learning to let go
> To allow the spiritual realities of this my life
>> To enter, to open and to control my life and living
> For Jesus is my Lord and Savior
>> He is becoming my way, my truth and my life

Thank You, Shepherd of my soul
> For so rich a pasture, so perfect the still waters
>> Which You have provided
>>> And will always provide

At this moment and for all eternity.

BOOKS FOR FURTHER READING

The Field by Lynne McTaggert
The Mozart Effect, by Don Campbell
Christian Thought Revisited, by Justo Gonzales
Quantum Reality, by Nick Herbert
Quantum Theory, by John Polkinghome
Language in Thought and Action, by S.I and Alan Hayakawa
The Portable Jung, collected by Joseph Campbell

OTHER BOOKS BY DR. ZILLMER

Are You My Friend?

An introduction to the first century message of Jesus

The Joys of the Lord

A daily devotional based on the writings of John.

I am the Morning Star

An in depth study of the 1ˢᵗ Century interpretation
of the book of Revelation. Scholarly research simply written
on the seven visions given for the aid and support of
Christians in times of persecution. Very different from
modern interpretations!

Images of Beauty

A daily devotional based on the 1ˢᵗ Century
interpretation of the book of Revelation.

Tuning in the Good Shepherd, 2 volumes

Daily devotions based upon a two year read through of the
entire Bible based upon twenty themes introduced in the first eleven
chapters of Genesis, developed in the Old Testament, climaxed in
Jesus life and teachings and concluded in the book of Revelation.

The Koran, Jesus Christ and Common Sense.

A simple, objective comparison of the Bible and the Koran based upon direct quotations from the Koran and the four Gospels.

Living With Agenda 21

An objective analysis of the United Nations socialist agenda, which, through executive order, is the law of our land, though most people have never heard of it, much less read or studied it! It is an expression of a modern anti-christ.

For further correspondence:

First Century Christian Fellowship,
10119 Gina Rd. Lindale, Tx. 75771,
Email: gostwing77@gmail.com,
903.881.0728

Edwards Brothers Malloy
Oxnard, CA USA
November 24, 2014